Persian Carpets

Persian Carpets

BY MICHAEL CRAIG HILLMANN

UNIVERSITY OF TEXAS PRESS, AUSTIN

Copyright © 1984 by the University of Texas Press
All rights reserved
Printed in the United States of America

First edition, 1984

Requests for permission to reproduce material from
this work should be sent to:
   Permissions
   University of Texas Press
   Box 7819
   Austin, Texas 78713

**Library of Congress Cataloging in
Publication Data**

Hillmann, Michael C.
   Persian carpets.
   Bibliography: p.
   Includes index.
   1. Rugs, Persian. I. Title.
NK2809.P4H53 1984 746.7'55 84-5185
ISBN 0-292-76490-1

For Sorayya

Contents

Illustrations

Preface and Acknowledgments

Because there are so many oriental carpet books on the market today, any new book needs to justify its existence with an explicit rationale for why another volume is being added to the already crowded oriental book shelf.

Persian Carpets is another introductory survey. But it is distinctive in at least two regards. First, it almost exclusively treats contemporary Persian carpets, that is to say, handwoven pile carpets produced in the country of Iran today. Second, the treatment involves aesthetic analysis and is from an Iranian studies point of view. In other words, the discussion focuses on evaluation of individual carpets as art in the context of their significance to Iran and Iranians.

Persian Carpets is intended for persons interested in oriental carpets who may not know a great deal about Iran, and for persons interested in Iran who may not know a great deal about Persian carpets.

This is a suggestive rather than conclusive study in terms of contemporary Persian carpets and Iranian society. It offers nothing startling or new for Iranologists or oriental carpet experts. But its suggestiveness, it is hoped, offers students of Iran, carpet *amateurs*, and neophytes alike data and bases for an appreciation of Persian carpet design possibilities, an ability to identify thirty or more of the most common Persian carpet types, and an awareness of the cultural significance of contemporary Persian carpet designs.

The first chapter is an introduction that describes the weaving of oriental carpets, introduces the reader to Iran, and considers the special significance of Persian carpets.

In the second chapter, carpets are discussed in terms of style, age, provenance, the subjects their designs include, and the designs themselves. In the third chapter, thirteen popular modern Persian carpet types are described to familiarize the reader with typical design possibilities.

The fourth and fifth chapters treat symbolism in modern Persian carpet designs and the relationship of Persian carpets and Iranian society. Seven additional modern Persian carpets are discussed in detail in these two chapters, and other designs are considered as well. The primary purpose is to suggest the cultural significance and richness of everyday contemporary Persian carpets.

The book concludes with a partially annotated bibliography based on a perusal of almost everything on the subject published since 1953. The annotations include the names of specific carpet types illustrated in the available books, including all those referred to but not illustrated in this volume.

The bibliography demonstrates that not a great deal of serious research on the subject of modern Persian carpets has been published. This means that much of the research for this book inevitably consisted of activity outside of libraries, involving assistance of various sorts for which I wish here to express gratitude.

Thanks go first to the Center for Middle Eastern Studies at the University of Texas at Austin for support of Persian carpet activities over the years, including the opportunity each summer to teach a course on the subject under its aegis. The University Research Institute at Texas has likewise supported my research on Persian carpets through summer and sabbatical grants, as has the Social Science Research Council. By means of their support, I was able to spend half of the summer of 1975 in Iran, part of the summer of 1976 visiting museums throughout North America, and half of 1982 in London.

I am grateful likewise to Austin's Laguna Gloria Museum Art School for inviting me to teach survey courses there on oriental rugs from the mid-1970s onward. The book is also the better from the experience afforded me through invitations to lecture in recent years at the Hajji Baba Society in New York, Loyola College in Baltimore, and Rice University in Houston. The day I spent talking about oriental carpets with Betty Rae Davis and her friends in Midland, Texas, was also particularly fruitful for me, as was the opportunity Janet Stoeltje of First National City Bank of Austin gave me to present a series of lectures to that institution's Great Expectations group.

Three oriental carpet dealers in Austin have been especially gracious in assisting my students and allowing me to study and photograph their carpets: Casey Waller of Caravanserai Carpets, Zahi Kaskas of Kaskas Oriental Rugs (Figs. 4, 11, 24, and 26), and Terence Carlman of The Magic Carpet. Jacobsen's in Syracuse has likewise been helpful (Figs. 17, 28).

Many of the carpets illustrated in this volume were part of the 1976 exhibition at the Huntington Gallery at the University of Texas at Austin. I want to thank the following individuals who lent their carpets to the exhibition and allowed them to be photographed: Mr. and Mrs. Leonard Bogle, Mr. and Mrs. Hafez Farmayan, Mr. and Mrs. Roger Hanks, Mr. and Mrs. David Inman, Curtis Jordan, Mr. and Mrs. John Peterson, William Smallwood, Mr. and Mrs. John A. Williams, and Mr. and Mrs. Gary A. Yarrington. Thomas Hartwell was the photographer. The Lyndon Baines Johnson Library also lent several carpets for showing in the exhibition, and Library photographer Frank Wolfe provided much appreciated photographs of LBJ carpets for inclusion in this volume (Figs. 5, 13, and 38).

I am also appreciative of the expert editing and indexing provided by Keith Walters. Special thanks go to Michael Jerald, with whom I shared many hours of investigating Persian carpets in Tehrān and on the road throughout Iran. I also need to thank my partners in our Caravan Carpets shop in Tehrān, especially Hossein Naraghy.

Finally and most importantly, there is my debt of gratitude to my wife Sorayya, who has been my partner in thinking and writing about Iranian culture since the mid-1960s. From *Unity in the Ghazals of Hāfez* (1976) to *Iranian Society: An Anthology of Writings by Jalāl Āl-e Ahmad* (1982) and from *An Iranian Woman Speaks (Out): The Life and Works of Forugh Farrokhzād* (forthcoming) to these Persian carpets, the sharing has been exciting and sustaining. We are still hoping that a day may come when we can be back in Iran doing it all over again.

Note on the Transcription of Persian Terms

Because Persian is not written in the roman alphabet as English is and because transcription systems vary from author to author, even such common place names as those which are cited in the checklist at the end of Chapter 2 are often problematic. The city of Qom is a good example; it is spelled many different ways in different carpet books, e.g., Qum, Qumm, Ghom, or Ghoum. In addition, there are technical and cultural terms in Persian that have no equivalent in English and thus need to be cited in a transcribed English form. Examples are *afshān*, *boteh*, and *gol*. John J. Wertime, "Some Suggestions Concerning the Spelling of Foreign Names and Terms in Oriental Carpet Literature," *Hali* 3 (1981): 210–213, discusses the whole question sensibly.

The transcription system used throughout this volume is presented below. The student of Persian carpets should learn it or some other system, perhaps one of his or her own devising, so as to be able to determine the correct pronunciation of relevant technical terms, place names, personal names, and other Persian words; to render Persian words accurately and systematically into English; and to determine what is intended in carpet literature in the use of Persian terms represented inaccurately or unsystematically in English. For more detailed information about the Persian sound system and alphabet, see Michael Hillmann, *The Fundamentals of Persian Reading and Writing* (Austin, Tex.: Persepolis Enterprises, 1983).

The following list includes all of the sounds which occur in the standard Tehrān dialect of Persian as they are represented throughout this book. After each English letter or pair of letters representing a Persian sound not immediately obvious to the speaker of English, an equivalent English sound is indicated in the cited English words. In cases for which there is no English equivalent, a brief explanation is provided.

ā	as in "p*o*d"
a	as in "p*a*d"
āy	as in "p*ie*"
ay	as in "p*ay*"
b	
ch	as in "*ch*ur*ch*"
d	
e	as in "b*e*t"
f	
g	as in "*g*ulf"
gh	see *q*
h	pronounced even in syllable-final and word-final positions, except in final ". . . eh," pronounced /e/
i	as in "b*ee*t"
j	as in "*j*elly"
k	
kh	not in English, same as "na*ch*t" in German
l	
m	
n	
o	as in "b*oa*st" (if pronounced without a "w" sound after the *oa*)
ow	as in "s*ew*"
p	
q & gh	not in English, same as "*q*iblah" in Arabic
r	not in English, same as Spanish "r"
s	
t	
u	as in "b*oo*st"
v	
y	
z	
'	glottal stop

All Persian nouns and adjectives are pronounced with the word accent or stress on their final syllable. For example: the name of the country is Irān, pronounced *ear* + *ón*, with a stress on *on*; the name of the capital city, Tehrān, is pronounced *te* + *h* (which is pronounced) + *rón*, with a stress on *ron*.

Persian Carpets

1. Introduction

The generally synonymous terms *oriental carpet* and *oriental rug* refer to specific kinds of hand-crafted floor coverings. All of them are the result of a process of weaving on a loom by means of passing widthwise weft threads through, alternately over and under, lengthwise warp threads. These warps are attached to upper and lower loom beams which serve to keep the warps taut and define the ultimate size and shape of the carpet.

The most common and important kind of oriental carpet is called *qāli* in Persian.[1] The Turkish word for the same fabric technique is the cognate *halı*, a term which may be of Iranian origin.[2] With a continuous history of production of at least four hundred years, *qāli* carpets have offered design possibilities that have resulted in floor coverings appreciated the world over as works of art.

Qāli-weaving

In precise terms, the *qāli* is a handcrafted fabric that combines the weaving of a foundation of warp and weft threads and the looping or hooking of tufts of material onto the warps, the ends of which tufts create a visible nap or pile. The procedures for producing such *qali* oriental carpets are basically the same wherever they are woven in whatever historical period, despite the use of different sorts of looms.[3]

First, warps are stretched and strung lengthwise all across the horizontal beams of the loom from top to bottom, thus forming from left to right the width of the final fabric. Second, two subsidiary rods or other devices are introduced to allow alternate vertical threads or warps to be raised or depressed so that the horizontal wefts may be readily woven over and under the warps across the carpet. Third, weft threads are woven horizontally into the strung warp threads to form a band of an inch or two at the bottom or beginning of the carpet. Fourth, a row of looped pieces of pile material, either wool or silk or a combination of the two, is introduced across the width of the carpet. Fifth, one or more wefts are introduced after each row of pieces of pile material is looped piece by piece across the carpet. The weaving of wefts is expedited by the use of the rods which are the length of the width of the carpet and to which are attached alternate warps. When either of the rods is lifted, a space is created across the width of the fabric through which a weft can be quickly passed. Sixth, each row of pieces of pile material together with subsequently woven wefts is beaten down evenly with a heavy, comb-like instrument. Seventh, procedures 4, 5, and 6 are repeated until the top end of the carpet is reached. Eighth, another band of woven wefts is formed at the top end of the carpet. Ninth, a selvage, which holds the warps and knots together along the lengthwise edges of the carpet, is woven with a loop stitch, overcasting of wefts, or other technique as work on the carpet proceeds. Tenth, the warp threads extending beyond the woven band at both ends of the carpet are untied or otherwise released from the loom, thus creating a fringe at both ends of the carpet. Eleventh, the pile, which has been partially clipped as work progressed, is evenly clipped.

---

1. Persian terms and expressions are used as defined by Mohammad Mo'in et al., *An Intermediate Persian Dictionary*, 6 vols. (Tehrān: Amir Kabir, 1977), unless otherwise indicated. The system used for spelling Persian terms and proper names in English is described in the Note on the Transcription of Persian Terms.

2. Joan Allgrove, "Bisāṭ" [Carpet, Rug], in *Encyclopaedia of Islam: New Edition, Supplement* (1981), p. 136.

3. Different sorts of Iranian looms are described by Arthur Cecil Edwards, *The Persian Carpet*, in the course of a discussion of "The Weaver's Craft," pp. 22–28. Hans E. Wulff, *The Traditional Crafts of Persia*, pp. 212–217, provides a standard definition of Persian *qāli* carpets and a description of the process by which they are produced.

The foundation of oriental carpets is the weave formed by warps, which can be cotton, cotton-wool, wool, or silk, and wefts, which can be cotton, wool, or silk. This foundation is not visible from the top side of the carpet except in the band of webbing at both ends of the carpet. The ends of the warps, of course, are visible as the fringe at both ends of the carpet. The visible design surface of the carpet is formed by the ends of the tufts of colored pile material, either wool or silk, introduced row by row across the carpet into the warps. The two most prevalent ways of looping the tufts of pile material are called the Persian knot and the Turkish knot.[4] (See Fig. 2.)

The Turkish knot consists of looping each tuft of pile material around the fronts of two adjacent warp threads and bringing the two ends of the piece up through the middle of the pair of warps, the two ends of the piece thus forming the pile. The Persian knot is formed, in either a left- or right-handed direction, by bringing the two ends of the piece of pile material around the same side, either left or right, of two adjacent warps; the wrapping of the two adjacent warps is, thus, one side over and the next under. Sometimes, both the Turkish and Persian knots are introduced into four warps rather than two. This procedure, called *jofti* or "doubled" knotting, reduces the density of the pile and consequently the durability of the carpet.

Another variation that can occur in oriental carpet-weaving is in the arrangement of the pairs of adjacent warps into which the tufts of pile material are introduced. The warp pairs can be on the same plane or one can be depressed vis-à-vis the other, even to the point of one being almost directly below the other. If every other warp is depressed, more warps can be wrapped across the loom, and the number of loops and consequent pile density thereby increased.

From the moment a loom is prepared for a carpet and a design is determined to the moment when that carpet appears somewhere for sale, a dozen or more persons have contributed to its production. If one traces the process back to the source of raw materials, complicated networks of

Figure 1. Tehrān weaver.

animal husbandry, craft, and merchandising become apparent. As of 1976, as many as one out of every thirty Iranians were involved in the production and sale of Persian carpets.[5]

These present-day techniques of oriental carpet-weaving continue traditions that originated many millennia ago in circumstances open to speculation.

Presumably, in Central Asia and perhaps as far west as the Iranian plateau, the dry, sometimes windy steppe and mountain climate, with its cold evenings all year round and especially cold winter days and nights, motivated early pastoral and hunting nomads, as well as villagers, to think about floor coverings for tents and huts.

The environment on the Iranian plateau and to the east provided an abundance of such floor covering materials as the skin and hair of wild animals and the skin, hair, and wool from sheep, goats, and camels. Hunting nomads presumably used the skin and hair of hunted animals as rugs. But pastoral nomads would be loathe to use ani-

4. John T. Wertime, "A New Approach to the Structural Analysis of the Pile Rug," *Oriental Rug Review* 3, no. 3 (June 1983): 12–16, presents an important new system for analyzing and describing *qāli* weaving, the precision of which is beyond the needs of this study. However, his demonstration of the fact that Persian and Turkish knots serve in their rows as a weft movement is important to bear in mind.

5. This is a conservative estimate. According to Jasleen Dhamija, *Living Tradition of Iran's Crafts*, p. 6, "Over a million people are involved in [Iranian] crafts, and if we were to take into consideration those who practice crafts for their personal needs the number is much larger." According to "Bohrān-e San'at-e Qāli-bāfi-ye Irān" [The Crisis in the Carpet-weaving Industry of Iran], *Irānshahr*, no. 184 (April 1, 1983): 5, five million Iranians, or 12 percent of the total population, have employment relating to carpet production.

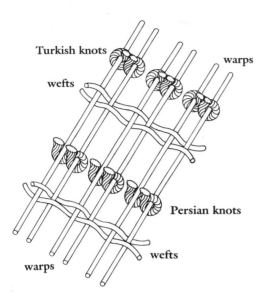

Figure 2. Persian and Turkish knots.

mal skin and hair together as floor covering. Doing so would have meant constant slaughtering of flocks, a source of dairy products and wool. Also, animal skins were needed for such other things as water bags, tent materials, and boots. The pastoral nomad may have first realized the potential supply of floor covering material in shorn wool that could be obtained regularly without detriment to the flock. These nomads presumably first produced mats, then woven floor coverings, and finally the combination of weaving and tufting or knotting characteristic of an oriental carpet. Some writers conclude, on this basis, that the knotted carpet originated in the mountain-traversed steppe belt in Asia, between roughly the thirtieth and forty-fifth latitude. South of that, the climate dictated the use of mats, and in the northern forests, the skins and attached hair of wild beasts provided the required floor covering.

The next step in the development of oriental carpets as historically known would have been the arranging of the pieces of pile material of the natural wool colors into patterns. In Iran today, natural wool color carpets are still produced in several places, notably Tabriz, Marand, Ardabil, Mashhad, and by the Qashqā'is. Then, once nomads and villagers began experimenting with natural dyes, the tufts would have been dyed to produce a design in colors other than the white-brown-grey-black spectrum of natural wool hues. A still further development was the shearing of the pile tufts after completion of the carpet so

that the shaggy appearance would be eliminated, and the pattern of the colored tufts would be clearer. These developments could have taken an extremely long time, and even when the final method of construction as it exists today became common, the product still must have been very different from what appears in the earliest extant carpets. Thus, whatever the oldest oriental carpets in a particular tradition turn out to be, hundreds or perhaps thousands of years of prior history must be assumed. Oriental carpet-making is a story of human ingenuity and resourcefulness, many details of which can only be surmised.

Still, the speculation here about the development of the process of oriental carpet-weaving as it has been known for the past 2,500 years does not answer perhaps more important questions about why the oriental carpet as it is today came into existence. As functional furniture, the solid, natural-color carpet was just as efficient as one in different natural wool colors or in other colors derived from plant and other dyes. Therefore, the question arises as to why early weavers first chose to produce designs with natural wool hues and later went to the trouble to dye the wool to create colored patterns in these pieces of furniture. One view is that "an innate aesthetic sense led to the ordering of the various natural wool colors into primitive patterns" and then subsequently to the use of dyed wool.[6]

Perhaps early weavers were proclaiming their individuality and sense of uniqueness through a designed and decorated floor covering. Through the ordering of colored decorative elements, weavers may have subconsciously striven to show at least to themselves either some understanding of order in the world around them or some control over it. They may have been trying to come to grips with meaning in their lives and in the world outside. Weavers may have found solace from the vicissitudes and sorrows of life in the self-expression of decorating a woven fabric. They may have been using color and the designs created by colors as a symbolic recognition of or tribute to forces of nature that played an important part in their lives. Or they may have been trying to leave something behind, to achieve a sort of permanence with this product of their creativity, skill, and imagination.

6. Reinhard Hübel, *The Book of Carpets*, p. 20. Hübel's speculations are behind parts of this and the several previous paragraphs.

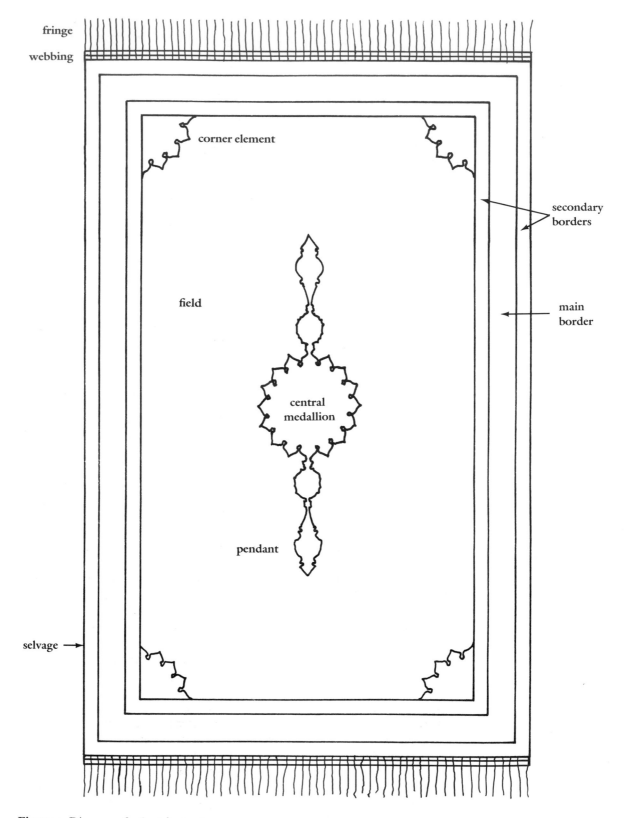

Figure 3. Diagram of oriental carpet components.

These rich, human dimensions to the development of oriental carpet-weaving are certainly part of the appreciation of modern Persian carpets. So are a further set of considerations that present themselves if the act of weaving itself is viewed as potentially symbolic. Accordingly, one sort of significance such crafts as carpet-weaving have is their contribution to the rhythm of life and to cosmic rhythm. The creative repetition that physically characterizes carpet-weaving is a rhythm of work that parallels such internal rhythms as inhalation-exhalation and biorhythm as well as exterior diurnal, tidal, seasonal, solar, and sidereal rhythms. This expression of harmony with physical nature is seen as a dimension not less significant than and parallel to the decoration of carpets that initially derived inspiration from physical nature in the weaver's attempts to achieve self-expression through the object he or she was making.[7]

The Country of Iran

The word *Persia* has come to English through Greek. It literally means "Pārs," today called "Fārs," the south central area of the Iranian plateau which was the capital province of the Persian Achaemenids, who ruled the great empire that lasted from 559 to 330 BCE (before the common era = B.C.). Arabicized forms of the word *Pārs* are the source of the word *Fārs* and of *Fārsi*, the name of the official language of Iran, usually referred to as "Persian" in English. Some dialect of Persian is spoken by the vast majority of Iranians as either a mother tongue or a second language.

In the Persian language, there is no equivalent for the term *Persia* that some non-Iranians, particularly the British, still use to refer to the country of Iran. As for the word *Irān*, it means "of or relating to Aryans." The first permanent settlers on the Iranian plateau were Indo-European Persians who moved westward into Iran in the tenth century BCE. Iranians themselves have always used the word *Irān* as the name of their homeland. Reza Shāh Pahlavi (1878–1944), founder of the short-lived Pahlavi dynasty (1925–1979) and father of Mohammad Rezā Pahlavi (1919–1980), proclaimed "Irān" as the official foreign designation for the country in the 1930s.

In reference to oriental carpets, the words *Persian* and *Iranian* are synonymous. There is no reason, except greater currency, for using *Persian* rather than *Iranian* in the title of this book. In fact, there may be two reasons against the appellation *Persian* in referring to the handcrafted pile carpets of Iran. First, for some people the phrase *Persian carpets* connotes exclusively the kinds of carpets exhibiting curvilinear elements and patterns which originated in the Safavid era (1501–1722). Carpets woven in Kermān with a central medallion on a plain, undecorated, single-color field are typical examples of curvilinear, floral designs from this period. On the other hand, many carpets exhibiting basically rectilinear elements and patterns, whether or not their inspiration derives from traditions originally beyond the borders of Iran, are equally Persian in the sense of being produced and used in Iran. Torkaman carpets with their patterns of repeated "geometric" shapes are typical examples of rectilinear designs woven in Iran today. Thus, the neutral term *Iranian* may more objectively describe all kinds of carpets woven in Iran.

Second, in linguistic and cultural terms, the word *Persian* is not always synonymous with *Iranian* in referring to inhabitants of Iran. Within Iran, one can speak of a "Persian" Iranian (called *Fārs* in Persian), a Turkish Iranian, an Armenian Iranian, a Kurdish Iranian, etc. In other words, an Iranian whose native language and culture are Persian, the dominant language and culture in Iran, is a "Persian" Iranian, whereas "Turkish" Iranians, who make up some 25 percent of the population of Iran, do not speak Persian as a native language but rather Āzarbāyjāni Turkish, and may or may not wholly share Persian Iranian culture. An Armenian in Iran, for example, has neither Persian as a native language nor the core Islamic element of Persian culture as part of his or her cultural identity. In similar ways, various tribal groups, who constitute over 5 percent of the population, are likewise Iranian but not necessarily Persian. Despite these considerations, the word *Persian* is used more than *Iranian* throughout this book in reference to pile carpets woven in the country of Iran. It is the more popular term, and few Iranian carpet types have been uninfluenced by Persian Iranian culture.

This book focuses almost exclusively on *qāli* carpets woven since the middle 1950s and intended as or amenable to use as floor coverings in private residences. Any attention given to older carpets is for the purpose of illuminating some salient aspect of contemporary Persian carpets and their use in Iran. Furthermore, items of carpet material which cannot be used as floor coverings, such as saddle bags, trunk covers, jug holders, cinches, and other decorative objects of

7. Dhamija, *Living Tradition of Iran's Crafts*, p. 67.

village and tribal production intended for quadrupeds or tents, go undiscussed here.

The designation of the middle 1950s may appear arbitrary as the starting point for the contemporary period of Iranian carpet production, since qāli-weaving is an industry with a definite, continuous history from the early years of the sixteenth century. But there are senses in which "contemporary Iran" as a combination of particular social circumstances can be said to have begun at about that time; these social circumstances have influenced qāli carpet production as well as use. In short, as different as the Iran of the second half of the 1950s may have been from the Iran of the 1960s and 1970s, Iranian society has seemed to be moving on a particular course charted and begun in the 1950s. It is today's Iran, with the importance it assumed in the early 1970s as an oil-rich nation and its post-Pahlavi significance as an Islamic Republic reacting against Westernization, that is of interest to people the world over who may or may not suspect that Iran's carpets can offer significant insights into that society.

With an area of more than 630,000 square miles, Iran is three times the size of France and more than twice the size of the American state of Texas. Its (mid-1980s) estimated population of forty-three million makes Iran one of the most populous countries in the Middle East. But Iran's physical environment and geographical location are quite different from those of any other country or region to which it can be compared in size or population. Its distinctiveness in these regards has doubtless influenced Iran's production and use of oriental carpets, as well as the nature of Persian carpet designs.

In general, Iran has four major physical zones. First is the Zāgros system of mountains and plains that extends from the northwest to the southeast and dominates the western half of the country. In the northern part of this region, Tabriz is the major urban center. In the south the major city is Shirāz.

Tabriz has nearly a million inhabitants and is the center of the Turkish-speaking region of Iran called Āzarbāyjān. Tabriz is the most obvious reminder of the fact that, although Persian and Persian Iranian culture have been dominant forces in Iran for millennia, Iran is a country of significant linguistic and cultural diversity. Another example is the Kordestān area to the south of Āzarbāyjān; it reaches across the borders into Turkey and Iraq. Not only do the Kurds, who number about

a million in Iran and whose weaving has been famous for a century, speak Kurdish, a language other than Persian, but their Sunni Moslem religion is also distinct from the Shi'i Moslem sect that controls the Iranian state and that has been Iran's official religion since the sixteenth century. In Āzarbāyjān, as well as in Tehrān and Esfahān, there are significant numbers of Armenian Iranians whose language and religion are also different from those of the dominant Persian Iranian group. Throughout Iran, there are Turkic and Iranian dialects that Persian speakers cannot understand.

The city of Shirāz at the southern end of the Zāgros is a quintessential Persian Iranian city. Its population is about 750,000. As the capital of the province of Fārs, Shirāz is typical of many Iranian urban centers as a hub around which village and tribal groups cluster. Shirāz is the marketplace of familiar Khamseh, Qashqā'i, and Lor textiles including flat-weave and qāli carpets woven by villagers and pastoralists who still participate in annual migrations in the region. More than 5 percent of the Iranian population is nomadic today, while more than 50 percent of the Iranian population lives in some sixty-seven thousand villages throughout the country.

A second geographical region in Iran is the Alborz system that extends from west to east in the northern part of the country and includes the Caspian plain. Its highest peak is Mount Damāvand, which, at nearly nineteen thousand feet above sea level, is the tallest mountain from Iran westward to the Atlantic Ocean. Located some forty miles northeast of Tehrān, Damāvand was clearly visible from the capital before thick air pollution became a problem there in the late 1960s.

On the north side of the Alborz mountains lie the Caspian lowlands. From Gilān, the westernmost of the two Caspian provinces, the caviar famous around the world is shipped. From the eastern part of Māzandarān, which is part of the Torkaman lowlands, come carpets with those familiar and important Torkaman designs.

Gilān and the western part of Māzandarān are the only areas of Iran that receive abundant rainfall. For most of Iran, the average annual precipitation is between one and six inches, almost all of it during the winter months. Consequently, almost all of Iran is arid, and its essential agricultural life is an arduous struggle to obtain water for the arable land.

The most important center to the south of the Alborz system is Tehrān. A village in the eigh-

Map 1. Iran.

teenth century, it became Iran's capital at the end of the century with the accession of the Qājār monarchs to the Iranian throne. By 1900 Tehrān had a population of 500,000. By the end of World War II, the population was 1,500,000. At the end of the Pahlavi era (1925–1979), Tehrān's population had reached 5,000,000. Typical of the situation in most Middle Eastern third world societies, Tehrān has become a city in almost total dominance of its country in political and economic terms. Inmigration, industry, government, and the like account for this. Socially and culturally, it is a separate living environment in the context of such second-tier cities as Mashhad, Esfahān, Shirāz, Tabriz, Rasht, and Ahvāz, third-tier cities such as Hamadān, Kermān, Birjand, Kāshān, and Yazd, smaller communities that one would label towns, the sixty-seven thousand or so villages, and the nine or so tribal areas. Tehrān's growth also points to another factor in Iranian life, its 3 percent annual population growth rate, which

means that Iran is doubling its population every twenty to twenty-five years.

A third physical zone in Iran is the interior plateau region that lies within the rim created by Iran's mountain systems. This region is composed of a number of inland basins that make up almost half of Iran's total land mass. Two features of the area that extends from Qom, the religious center of Iran more than ninety miles south of Tehrān, to Kermān, the important south-central city over four hundred miles from the capital, are typical of the whole country. First is its aridity. Second is the uninhabitability of much of the interior plateau area, principally the desert basins called Dasht-e Kavir to the east of Qom and Dasht-e Lut to the east of Kermān. In general, only about 10 percent of Iran's territory is arable and habitable. Consequently, the population density of the inhabited parts of Iran is relatively high in spite of the size of the country.

The most important city in the interior plateau

is Esfahān, located in a fertile valley of the Zāyandeh River halfway between Tehrān and Shirāz. Esfahān, in fact, is the only Iranian plateau city located on such a river. However, as important as the Zāyandeh River is, it is not navigable. This is another feature of Iran in general: there are almost no rivers to link urban centers to each other or to seas.

With a population of one million people, Esfahān has long been Iran's favorite tourist site, owing to its Safavid architecture, avenues, and the bridges across its famous river. The Chahār Bāgh Avenue, the Shāh Square, Siyoseh Pol bridge, and Jāme' Mosque, among others, are well-known examples of another physical feature of much of Iran: the presence of evidence of history in the form of ruins, caravanserais, mosques, fortresses, and archaeological sites. Iranians are reminded at every turn of their country's history and of the significance of religion and monarchy in it.

The principal settlement in the southeastern part of these interior basins is Kermān, capital of Kermān province and a city of some 150,000 people. Its vicissitudinous history is typical of many Iranian cities. Founded in the third century as a defensive outpost of the Persian Sāsānian empire (224–640 CE), Kermān was converted to Islam during the first quarter of the eighth century and became an important regional city during the tenth century, when it served as a provincial capital of the Persian Sāmānid empire. The Kermān region prospered under Saljuq rule during the eleventh century and, owing to its remoteness, escaped the Mongol invasion in 1220. At the end of the thirteenth century, Marco Polo visited it and later recorded comments on swords and other weapons made there. A century later Kermān was conquered by the armies of Tamerlane (1335–1405). During the Safavid era (1501–1722), Kermān again prospered, in part because of its location on an Indo-Iranian highway. Its shawls and embroidery were famous. Persian carpet-weaving developed there during the reign of Shāh 'Abbās the Great (1587–1629). Afghān tribesmen conquered Kermān twice in the 1720s and again in 1747. Before the latter invasion, Nāder Shāh Afshār had caused a seven-year famine in the region by requisitioning all of the area's agricultural surplus to support his military campaigns in Afghanistan. In 1794, as the Qājārs were beginning to assert control over all of Iran, they overcame Kermān in routing the last Zand leader. In the process they blinded twenty thousand men and sold another twenty thousand into slavery.

The fourth zone is the upland-rim area of the eastern and southeastern regions of the country. The province of Baluchestān and Sistān, bordering Pakistan and the Persian Gulf, is to the south and includes some of the most forbidding living environments in all of Iran. The traditional home of Iranian Baluch tribal people is in this region. The largest city in the area is Zāhedān, a recently developed urban center intended to serve as the Iranian conduit for trade with Pakistan. Over two hundred miles north of Zāhedān, in the province of Khorāsān, is Birjand, the largest urban center in the eastern section of the country. Then about an equal distance north of Birjand lies the most important city in the Iranian east, Mashhad, a city of over a million people. The size and vitality of Mashhad are testimony to the essential significance of religion to Iran. The name Mashhad means "place of the martyr." The city grew because an important ninth-century religious leader is buried there. Throughout Iran, there are villages and towns whose *raison d'être* is an association with a religious event or personage. Religion thus has a physical presence in Iran as real as the great mountains, broad plains, and vestiges of invasions and ruins of empires.

The province of Khorāsān, of which Mashhad is the capital, is geographically typical of much of the Iranian plateau in that it is prone to earthquakes. A September 1968 earthquake wiped out Ferdows, a town with a population of perhaps ten thousand at that time. Another devastating earthquake hit the region in 1978. The topography in Khorāsān and other places in Iran is also conducive to seasonal flooding caused by melting snow at higher elevations and to avalanches that regularly occur in several mountain pass regions of the country. The mountains and plateau of Iran also give the country a difficult climate. One of only a few countries in the world with an average elevation of three thousand feet above sea level, most of Iran experiences extremely hot summer days and cold winters.

There are, however, regions in Iran that do not fit this general pattern. For example, the Caspian littoral, which averages three hundred feet above sea level, receives an annual rainfall in excess of twenty inches; consequently, it is greener than the rest of the country. A second exception is the outer edge of the Zāgros system down toward Ahvāz in Khuzestān, which might be viewed as part of Mesopotamia rather than as part of the

Iranian plateau. Interestingly, in such areas *qāli*-weaving is less important than it is on the plateau. This putative connection between the significance of *qāli*-weaving and Iran's plateau environment seems to hold throughout the rest of the Middle East. The craft is an important indigenous phenomenon in Turkey, the Caucasus, and Afghanistan in regions similar physically and geographically to the general pattern in Iran. On the other hand, *qāli*-weaving is not an important craft in the very different environments of Arab Moslem desert cultures.

If Iran's physical appearance and structure are distinctive and presumably influential in shaping Iranian society, culture, and such crafts as *qāli* carpet-weaving, Iran's geographical location is no less so. The Iranian plateau is an important land bridge between East and West, a corridor and crossroads of great historical significance. In this context, Iran's three thousand years of history can be described as the efforts of the Iranian people to deal with a series of invasions.

First came the invasion of Alexander the Great and his Greek armies in 330 BCE; this brought to an end the Persian Achaemenid empire. It was followed by some Hellenization of the region. Second was the invasion of the Moslem Arabs that ended the Sāsānian empire of Iran in the middle of the seventh century CE. The Arab invasion, the most important event in Iranian history, brought to Iran a new religion that is espoused by 95 percent of the Iranian population over 1,300 years later. The third major invasion was that of two waves of Mongols in the middle of the thirteenth century. Jenghis Khan's hordes wreaked devastation from which some communities in Iran never recovered. The fourth and most recent invasion has been an ongoing Western one that commenced in the eighteenth century. Czarist Russia, the British, and more recently the Americans have been the invaders this time. The post–World War II American invasion was not military but economic and cultural in nature. Throughout the 1960s and 1970s, many Iranians expressed great fears that the Americanization of Iran might bring Iranian culture to an end. The Khomayni revolution and the establishment of the Islamic Republic of Iran in the spring of 1979 put an end to this threat from the West for the time being.

Iran's location as a crossroads between East and West, the ruggedness of its terrain, its unusual elevation, the aridity, changeability, and harshness of its climate, and its distinctive history make it a special social environment and perhaps even define it as a society. In that society, Persian carpets are themselves special and in some ways contribute to that definition.

The Special Significance of Persian Carpets

Persian carpets are both heir to and part of traditions that extend from the Western Mediterranean to the Far East. Some Persian city carpets from various parts of the country show the influence of Chinese art upon Middle Eastern Islamic art. Motifs and patterns from Turkish carpet traditions have been an important influence on various carpet types associated with villages and towns in Iranian Āzarbāyjān. Conscious borrowing and adaptation of elements of Caucasus design traditions are evident in modern Persian carpets from Ardabil and Meshkinshahr. Finally, the great Central Asian Torkaman design traditions are an important part of Torkaman and Baluch weaving in eastern and northeastern Iran.

There are six prominent and distinct geographical traditions in oriental carpet production: Turkey, the Caucasus, Iran, Central Asia, the Indian subcontinent, and China. In the contemporary period, Romania must be added to the list, Pakistan and India distinguished, and Afghanistan appreciated as separate from both Iranian and Central Asian spheres.

There are several reasons why special attention might be paid to Persian carpets. First, among the major oriental carpet-weaving traditions, Persian carpets exhibit the greatest variety in sizes, shapes, materials, grades, motifs, and patterns. As a survey of the most popular carpet types woven in Iran today reveals, Persian carpets represent almost the range of oriental carpets in general, both historically and geographically. Second, the great variety in design makes Persian carpet production a microcosm of oriental carpet weaving. Third is the fact that carpet production in Iran is not primarily for export. Nowhere in the world are oriental carpets more important in daily life than in Iran. Persian carpets are woven on migrations, in villages, towns, and cities, and in fields, yards, private homes, and large factories throughout Iran. They are used by nomads as floorcoverings in tents. They are underfoot during daily ritual Moslem prayers. They are found everywhere, in hovels and palaces, in dingy slum rooms, in high-rise apartments and villas, in government offices and hotels. They are a first concern of Iranian newlyweds about to set up household and the inevitable gift of Iranian leaders to heads of foreign states. They are sold in fancy hotel emporia, hawked by villagers door-to-door in north Tehrān, and purchased and stuffed under beds by Iranian investors as a hedge against inflation. They are the single most important piece of furniture and art in Iranian homes of all kinds and, likewise, Iran's most important industrial art.

A fourth reason for special attention to Persian carpets is their distinctive aesthetic appeal, which has been recognized in the West for the four centuries from which carpets are extant, at least by the many European painters who have depicted them in their works.[8] The basis for Western artists' appreciation of Persian carpets has essentially been their appeal in terms of composition and colors. Persian carpets exhibit techniques of color combination which painters have apparently tried to fathom by experimenting with them. As an example of the appeal Persian carpets have had for painters, Eugène Delacroix once declared that they were the most beautiful pictures he had ever seen.[9] Such fascination is one sort of expert testimony to Persian carpets as an art form.

Such testimony is helpful because scholars of Persian carpets and other experts provide little aesthetic commentary or criticism in their writing on carpets.[10] The importance of considering the aesthetics of Persian carpets is further accentuated by the fact that most Persian carpet owners and *amateurs* do not often seem comfortable or confident in describing impressions of aesthetic features of the carpets despite the fact that visual appeal is obviously among the things that attract them to the carpets.

Now one's impressions of individual carpets or reactions to carpets in general may ultimately be quite subjective in important ways. But with basic knowledge of Persian carpets, recognition

of criteria for evaluation in such a medium, and a dispassionate and consistent vocabulary for verbalizing responses to individual carpets, such impressions may be objective or at least evaluative in important senses. Even after a cursory introduction to Persian pile carpet-weaving, one has criteria of technical sorts pertaining to shapes, color, and design by which to evaluate a particular Persian carpet with the expectation that others would agree that it is a failure or a success as a carpet.

For example, if the color of a section of a carpet is not identical with the rest—a problem called abrash, usually caused by lots of pile not dyed at the same time or by different wool lots dyed the same color—this causes an observable irregularity in the field color or in a group of motifs that surely affects the carpet's appearance. If a particular design element, a stylized flower for example, is crowded next to another element or unfinished, that too affects the carpet's appearance and appeal. In a carpet field pattern depicting animals, some of which are bound to appear upside-down depending upon where the observer is when viewing the carpet, the carpet fails as a design if it does not integrate the animal shapes into the rest of the pattern so as to be ignored when upside-down. A final example, among scores of possible objective flaws in carpet designs, is lack of continuity in a border design that promises at first glance to circumscribe the field pattern in its rectangular confines. A weaver's miscalculation of width, especially in memorized designs as opposed to those woven from cartoons, may cause breaks in motifs or in the movement of the border around corners at any edge except the one at which weaving was begun. This again is a clear flaw that affects the aesthetic appeal, furniture attractiveness, and commercial value of the carpet.

---

8. Ian Bennett, ed., *Complete Illustrated Rugs and Carpets of the World*, presents over twenty plates of fifteenth-through-eighteenth-century paintings that depict Saljuq and Ottoman Turkish, Persian, and Caucasian carpets.

9. David Sylvester, "On Western Attitudes to Eastern Carpets," in *Islamic Carpets from the Joseph V. McMullan Collection*, pp. 4, 6.

10. Ian Bennett, "Editorial," *Hali* 1 (1978): 109–110. Among the few primarily aesthetic discussions of oriental carpets are the following: Myrna Bloom, "An Analysis of a Sarouk Prayer Rug—Its Pictorial and Textural Qualities," *Hali* 2 (1979): 162–164; Heinz Meyer, "The Carpet as a Work of Art," in *Rare Oriental Carpets IV*, ed. Jon Thompson and Eberhart Herr-

mann (Munich: Eberhart Herrmann, Teppich-Antiquitaten, 1982), reviewed by John J. Collins, Jr., *Oriental Rug Review* 2, no. 5 (August 1982): 8–9, 11; George O'Bannon, "A Modest Proposal: Aesthetics and the Judging of Oriental Weavings," *Oriental Rug Review* 2, no. 8 (November 1982): 6–7, which presents "a system . . . patterned on other types of things which people own, collect . . . and spend large amounts of money on; in short, the competitions for honors at flower, cat, dog, and horse shows"(!); Hans-Günther Schwarz, "Die Ästhetik des Persischen Teppichs," *Hali* 3 (1980): 137–138; and Eric Schroeder, "The Art of Looking at Rugs," in *McMullan Exhibition* (Cambridge, Mass.: Fogg Art Museum, 1949), pp. 4–13.

Map 2. Iranian carpet-weaving regions, centers, and peoples.

Appeal as furniture has been an important aspect of the special significance of Persian carpets. Here too lies a whole series of aesthetic concerns. For example, as one critic puts it:

To spend half a minute looking at a rug is to waste half a minute, for the object was made to be considered at leisure, and in the mood of rest. Arabesques are meant to be followed. Series of tones may be observed at first in a like kinaesthetic fashion, by remarking the use of tone at its allotted intervals, some green or rose reintroduced as leaf, stripe, flower and so on, in a different environment and shape. There is constant appeal to the circumference of vision and the eye resting on one place should not be too definitely centered, for it is in the "tail of the eye" that the most interesting recognitions of design will be found.[11]

A Persian carpet functions completely as art with the extra-utilitarian aspects described in the quotation only when it is on the floor in a room setting as furniture. Thus, principles of interior design in general and floor covering design in particular are part of the special significance of Persian carpets as art.

In furniture terms, a Persian carpet is a floor insulator against cold, a protective cover that increases traction and cushions falls, a surface that can be soft enough to sit on, a deterrent to airborne noise, a factor in reducing leg and foot fatigue, and, depending upon how light it is, a reflector of light that can thus brighten a room. All these practical concerns may seem little related per se to Persian carpets as art, but the distinctions between the concerns of art and those of furniture are not clear-cut. For example, the lightness and brightness of carpet colors are furniture aspects in effecting warmth and greater lightness in a room and aesthetic aspects in effecting pattern and in harmonizing with other furnishings in the room. Similarly, the placement of

---

11. Schroeder, "The Art of Looking at Rugs," pp. 10–12.

particular carpets of particular sizes in rooms can help determine how persons will move about and through rooms as well as how they will group themselves in conversation. This furniture concern is paralleled with how such placement affects the viewing of carpets, an aesthetic concern. The long-term appeal of a Persian carpet, an important aesthetic concern, is obviously as important a furniture concern. If the colors and pattern of a particular Persian carpet are determinants of pleasure for the carpet viewer in terms of its art, those features, together with the dimension of texture, are as significant in furniture terms in contributing to the mood of the area in which it is placed. The conventional presence of borders relates to room shape; a means of integrating the carpet into a room, of bringing the lines of the walls and ceiling and floor into focus centering upon the carpet in the room is the use of repeated lines parallel to floor, wall, and ceiling lines. Once this balance and movement of line are created, the presence in the border of color

and design elements repeated in the field of the carpet attract the attention of the viewer to the area framed by the border. Such considerations are a further reminder that even in the most aesthetic sort of response to Persian carpets, a carpet exists in all its dimensions only when it is on the floor in a room setting.

Other various furniture concerns or aspects have to do with room setting for the carpet—living room, dining room, or bedroom; the surface on which the carpet is to be placed—on a wall as a wall hanging, on floors that may be wood, marble stone, tile, linoleum, or covered with machine-made wall-to-wall carpeting; the colors of the walls, floor, ceiling, and other furniture; the style of the other furniture; and the amount of space to be covered.[12]

12. A. S. Whiton, "Floor Coverings," in *Interior Design and Decoration*, 4th ed. (Philadelphia: Lippincott, 1974), pp. 474–503, provides a comprehensive discussion of rugs as floor coverings.

2. Identification and Classification of Persian Carpets

Visual comparison of almost any oriental carpet with a machine-made pile carpet quickly reveals the differences in their construction. First, if one looks down the shafts of pile material toward the foundation of the carpet, the looping or knotting of tufts of pile material onto pairs of adjacent warps in an oriental carpet will be easily distinguishable from the stitching or gluing of pile material to the carpet's foundation in a machine-made carpet. Second, the fringe on an oriental rug consists of the ends of the warp threads cut from the upper and lower loom beams and disappears into the webbing or pile at the top and bottom ends of the carpet, whereas on a machine-made carpet the fringe is either sewn onto the carpet or overcast beyond the pile area. Third, the selvages of an oriental carpet are often wefts that are overcast beyond the last warp and wrapped with a piece of pile material, while machine-made carpets generally feature stitched selvages. Fourth, looking at the backside of a machine-made carpet, one sees precise uniformity of weaving as opposed to the wavy or otherwise slightly irregular rows of pile knots and visible wefts on the back of an oriental carpet. Fifth, on the back side of an oriental carpet one sees a distinct image of the carpet's design interrupted only by the appearance of lines of wefts in coarsely woven pieces, whereas on the back side of a machine-made carpet the carpet's design is never clearly visible and is sometimes not visible at all because of a layer of backing attached to the carpet.[1]

Style

Probably the most striking visual difference observable among Persian carpets of various sizes, shapes, and colors is that between two distinctive treatments of motifs and patterns. On the one hand, many motifs and patterns are geometric or rectilinear. Popular Torkaman, Baluch, and Caucasus-inspired Persian carpets from Ardabil and Meshkinshahr are obvious examples of such motifs and patterns. In contrast, many motifs are relatively naturalistic and their patterns curvilinear. The familiar Kermān floral medallion with plain field carpet, Tabriz hunting carpets, garden scene carpets from Esfahān, Nā'in, Qom, and elsewhere, and medallion carpets with obviously floral fields from throughout Iran are common examples of curvilinear Persian carpets.

Common to the major types of rectilinear design carpets, with one or two exceptions, is the weaver's reliance on memory as opposed to reference to a cartoon of the sort typically used for carpets with a curvilinear pattern. In the case of the rectilinear design carpets, the weaver typically learns the whole repertoire of motifs, overall field and border patterns as an apprentice under supervision. A daughter, for example, works with her mother. Later she begins producing one or two types of carpets, the overall pattern of which, perhaps including borders, is set; for the introduction of such secondary motifs as floral scatter, she relies on intuition. This sort of weaving is well illustrated by Qashqā'i and Khamseh carpets in which the central medallion and corner elements, together with a large polygon defining the field area, are predetermined, but the placement of smaller floral and stellate shapes is somewhat spontaneous or random. In terms of the sophistication of the weaver of such carpets, such weaving is analogous to oral formulae of folk literature in which, while following a basic story line, the individual storyteller embellishes details with stock devices, so that no two redactions of a particular orally transmitted tale are exactly the same. This mixture of constraints and choice makes many Persian carpets anonymous in one

---

1. The visible differences between oriental and machine-made carpets are described by Janice Summers Herbert, *Affordable Oriental Rugs: The Buyer's Guide to Rugs from China, India, Pakistan, and Romania* (New York: Macmillan, 1980), pp. 140–142.

sense. Yet at the same time, they show the imprint of the individual Qashqā'i or Afshār weaver in those minor aspects of design which permit spontaneity.

Obviously, the classification of Persian carpets as curvilinear, rectilinear, or a combination of the two is an important concern in furniture terms, since different carpet styles suit different styles in other furnishings. It is of sociological significance as well insofar as rectilinear motifs and designs were originally associated with tribal weaving and curvilinear ones with urban weaving; such hybrid designs as popular Hamadān, Heris, and Josheqān types were generally woven in smaller cities in which there have been some village or tribal influences.

Age

A second important way of classifying Persian carpets is according to their age. There are no known extant Persian carpets which predate the Safavid era (1501–1722). Therefore, the first category of antique Persian carpets consists of classical antiques from the sixteenth through the nineteenth centuries. In other words, a classical antique Persian carpet is one woven at some time during the period which began with the Safavids and ended during the Qājār dynasty (1796–1925). A second period of Persian carpets includes antique carpets produced from about 1900 to 1930, the latter years of the Qājār era and the first years of the Pahlavi era (1925–1979). Some experts use the term *semi-antique* in referring to older Persian carpets up to fifty years of age. The end of Mosaddeq's premiership (1951–1953) is a convenient stopping point for carpets in this category; consequently, semi-antiques would include Persian carpets woven during the 1930s, 1940s, and early 1950s. The fourth and final period used for dating Persian carpets coincides with the post-Mosaddeq years of Mohammad Rezā Pahlavi's rule and the subsequent Islamic Republic era, which began in the spring of 1979. Although they are here and there called "new" or "modern," among them are carpets that may not in fact be brand new or unused.

Of course, the dating of Persian carpets depends upon the use of data from other kinds of classification systems, such as the nature of the weave, the number and kind of weft threads, the structure of the pairs of warps used in the introduction of each piece of pile material, the wool or silk pile material itself, and the nature and intricacy of designs that underwent evolution

and change during various periods. Such technical aspects of weaving have been treated in detail elsewhere.[2]

The classification of Persian carpets according to age is naturally of primary importance to art historians, museum curators and researchers, and collectors. But it should also be important to *amateurs* and investors whose main interest is in new Persian carpets because many modern carpets exhibit basically traditional patterns. Familiarity with the history of various types of Persian carpets leads to an appreciation of how contemporary designers and weavers use and adapt traditional techniques, colors, motifs, and patterns.

PRE-MODERN HISTORY OF PERSIAN CARPETS

The known history of oriental carpet-weaving dates from nearly 2,500 years ago some 2,000 miles to the northeast of present-day Iran in the Pazyryk Valley of the Altai Mountain region of southern Siberia. There, in 1949, a Russian archaeologist discovered a carpet 200 × 183 cm in size with Turkish knots in a Scythian burial mound. Known as the Pazyryk carpet, this rug, as well as other carpet fragments with Persian knots found in the same tomb, is datable to the fifth century BCE. At Bashādar, some 180 km west of where the Pazyryk carpet was discovered, the same archaeologist discovered in another Scythian tomb a more finely woven carpet fragment with Persian knots; the fragment, which had been used in a saddle, is datable to 150 years before the Pazyryk carpet.[3]

The Pazyryk carpet exhibits the conventional division of design elements into field and border areas. The field consists of a checkerboard or compartment pattern of quatrefoil floral motifs surrounded by five borders. The largest border shows a counterclockwise procession of horsemen and grooms mounted on or walking by their horses. The second-largest border features a clockwise frieze of elk or reindeer. Between these two main borders are quatrefoil motifs similar to

---

2. E.g., Peter Collingwood, *The Techniques of Rug Weaving* (New York: Watson-Guptill, 1978); and Irene Emery, *The Primary Structures of Fabrics* (Washington, D.C.: Textile Museum, 1980).

3. Sergei Rudenko, *Frozen Tombs of Siberia*, trans. M. W. Thompson, features illustrations and discussion of the Pazyryk carpet. Recent discussions include Nejat Diyarbekirli, "New Light on the Pazyryk Carpet," *Hali* 1 (1978): 216–221, and Lemyel Amirian, "The Pazyryk Rug: Another View," *Oriental Rug Review* 1, no. 8 (November 1981): 7–8.

those in the field. The two outer borders feature griffins enclosed in nearly square shapes. The various border elements show a mixture of Assyrian, Scythian, and Persian motifs.

Because the arrangement and shapes of the field motifs are similar to those found on alabaster slabs presumably representing carpets on the floors of palaces of Assyrian rulers Sennacherib (705–681 BCE) and Assurbanipal (688–626 BCE) at Nineveh, some experts argue that the Pazyryk carpet is a product of the Middle East.[4] Because the main border depicts a scene of horsemen not unlike the processions of representatives from tributary states paying homage to the Persian Achaemenid emperor found in some bas-reliefs at Persepolis and because the griffins seem Archaemenid as well, some scholars believe that the Pazyryk carpet is either of Iranian origin or made in honor of the Persian empire.[5] No matter what its true origin, the Pazyryk carpet is extremely important in the study of Persian carpets for two reasons. First, its sophistication implies a long tradition which may never be known. Second, many of its features, not the least important being that the field represents a formal garden, have since remained part of the tradition.

At the beginning of the Sasānian era (224–640) or perhaps a century or more earlier, another important chapter in the history of oriental rugs began. Evidence for this development is the fragments discovered in the 1920s by a British Museum excavation at Lou-lan, a town in Chinese Turkestan. These fragments, which date from the fifth or sixth century CE, are woven in Turkish and Spanish knots. Their existence constitutes the basis for the view that "the knotting of pile carpets was a well-developed and frequently encountered art form in East Turkestan–Mongolia long before it migrated west."[6] But another view asserts that the provenance of these fragments is unknown and that "Perhaps they were made lo-

cally, perhaps they were imported from the west, possibly from eastern Persia . . . which was under Sasanian rule during the centuries mentioned . . . and had active trade relations with Chinese Turkestan."[7] Furthermore, other fragments of pile carpets from early Sāsānian days with Persian and Turkish knots were discovered in 1922 by a Yale University expedition in excavations at Dura-Europas, an ancient Syrian city on the Euphrates. Finally, dating from late Sāsānian days, come two fragments found in Egypt. Both exhibit the Spanish knot and were presumably the work of Christian Copts.

The most famous of the Sāsānian kings was Khosrow, often called Chosroe in English. During his reign, which ended in 579, the last cultural and artistic flourishes of the great Sāsānian empire occurred. More important to the history of oriental carpets is the association of Khosrow with a garden carpet of incredible dimensions that supposedly adorned the royal palace in Ctesiphon. Of this sumptuous piece, allegedly studded with pearls and gems and brocaded with gold and silver thread, nothing has survived. Nor is it clear that it was in fact an example of the pile carpet technique. This lack of certainty about the kind of carpet material being referred to is also true of the earlier documentary evidence concerning carpet production in the Old and New Testaments and in Greek and Roman appreciation of "Babylonian" carpets.

In connection with the Khosrow "spring" carpet, one notes several significant things. One is the unlikelihood of discovering other carpets from long ago, not only because of the perishability of carpet materials, but also because of such historical phenomena as repeated devastation through invasion and war, and violent changes in dynasties, part of which often included the destruction of the previous ruler's goods. A second is the longstanding tradition of the garden carpet, used in Khosrow's case specifically as a reminder of the beauty of spring in winter months. The third concerns a tradition of symbolism in some carpets. According to *Encyclopaedia Britannica*, the Khosrow carpet "symbolized the divine role of the king, who regulated the seasons and guaranteed spring's return, renewing the earth's fertility and assuring prosperity. On another plane, it represented the Garden of Eden, a symbol of eternal paradise . . . with its flowers, birds,

4. A photograph of a stone pavement slab from the north palace of Assurbanipal at Nineveh, ca. 640 BCE, at the British Museum, appears in Ian Bennett, ed., *Complete Illustrated Rugs and Carpets of the World*, p. 41.

5. Reinhard Hübel, *The Book of Carpets*, p. 15.

6. Bennett, ed., *Complete Illustrated Rugs and Carpets of the World*, p. 39. A third sort of pile knotting is called the Spanish knot and consists of looping an individual piece of pile material around a single warp. Because every other warp is left without a knot, the pile density is the same as with the usual manner of tying Persian and Turkish knots.

7. Maurice S. Dimand, *Oriental Rugs in the Metropolitan Museum of Art*, p. 6.

and water, it symbolized deliverance from the harsh desert and the promise of eternal happiness."[8] These traditions, which perhaps persist in contemporary Persian carpets, were reinforced on the Iranian plateau by the Moslem civilization which followed the Sāsānian period.

Although there is a great deal of evidence of oriental rug-weaving on the Iranian plateau and neighboring areas from the advent of Islam onward, it is with the Saljuqs, who entered the Iranian plateau in the eleventh century, that the history of the oriental carpet takes up again after the Sāsānian period. The Saljuqs seem to have brought westward a carpet-weaving tradition that became widespread in what is today the country of Turkey. Marco Polo, traveling eastward in 1271, recorded his wonder at the beauty of the Saljuq carpets of Turkey. Eight thirteenth-century fragments of Saljuq carpets were discovered in 1905 in the Alā' al-Din Mosque in Konya, built in 1220. Later, in 1929, three Saljuq rugs were discovered among a larger group of rugs in the Eshrefoglu Mosque built in 1296 at Beyshehir southwest of Konya. Finally, in 1935 and 1936, seven fragments of Saljuq carpets were discovered among the ruins of Fostat or Old Cairo in Egypt. All of these Saljuq carpets are relatively coarsely woven in Turkish knots in an all-wool fabric. The great size and elaborateness of design of some of them imply that oriental rugs as produced by the Saljuqs were an important craft in the thirteenth century.[9] Although no Saljuq rugs or fragments of Iranian origin are known, the existing Saljuq pieces from Turkey represent the same tradition, if similarities in other Saljuq arts of the two areas are any indication. These nearly twenty carpets or fragments are designed with rectilinear elements and feature a diaper of half-rows on the field "achieved by an endless repetition of the same isolated motif (octagon, hooked lozenge) or by a lattice-like arrangement of lozenges or star rosettes connected by strongly linear interlaced stems which gives the effect of an independent motif. The dominant motifs are almost always in lighter tones of the dark blue, red or dark red-brown ground of the central field. Characteristic of the broad borders are heavy wedge-shaped hooks derived from the stylization of Kufic script of rows of rosettes geometricized

Figure 4. Ardabil Lotto design carpet.

to squares."[10] Thus, these Saljuq carpets represent one of the persisting traditions in Persian carpets.

The Safavid dynasty, which ruled Iran from 1501 till 1722, is generally associated with the presumed "golden age" of Persian carpet-weaving. Actually, the Safavids were rulers of a middle kingdom between the Ottoman empire in Turkey and the Mughal empire in the Indian subcontinent.

In Turkey, from the Saljuq era down into the Ottoman empire, important developments in the designs of oriental carpets took place. Some of the available information about these developments comes from surviving carpets, and much comes from European paintings of Turkish carpets beginning with an early-fourteenth-century fresco by Giotto in the Arena Chapel in Padua. Among the latter are the Holbein and Lotto carpet types that appeared in paintings by other painters as well, but have become famous from their depiction in paintings by Hans Holbein the Younger and Lorenzo Lotto. The overall repeat

8. "Rugs and Carpets," *Encyclopaedia Britannica*, 15th ed. (1974).

9. Dimand, *Oriental Rugs in the Metropolitan Museum of Art*, p. 19.

10. Hübel, *The Book of Carpets*, pp. 19–20.

pattern of polygon *gol* shapes in the Holbein carpet seems a prototype for modern Torkaman carpets. The lattice effect of angular vines and arabesques on a plain field in the Lotto carpet type also survives today in some Meshkinshahr and Ardabil carpets, albeit in very different colors, often an off-white network of vines and arabesques on a dark blue field. (See Fig. 4.)

Among important surviving Ottoman Turkish carpet patterns is one with the design known as Star Ushāk, a symmetrical arrangement of two large stellate shapes that disappear under the borders, effecting a sense of an infinite galaxy of such shapes. Variations of this pattern can be found among modern Persian carpets from Esfahān and Nā'in. (See Fig. 5.)

Another Ottoman type of carpet is the famous Transylvanian carpet, so called because early examples were found in churches there. It features a field divided into two areas by a large diamond or hexagonal figure of one color around which the triangular shapes of the corners of the field are represented in another field color. Often these Transylvanian carpets are referred to as double-arch or double-niche carpets because both ends of the field with its arch and spandrels have reminded some observers of the arch-shape that causes the one-directionality of prayer carpet designs. The division of the field space into two areas with a diamond or hexagonal polygon remains a common design feature in such contemporary Persian carpet types as Ābādeh, Qashqā'i/ Khamseh, Mazlaqān, Afshār, and the like.[11]

All of these historically significant Turkish carpet types, as well as later and likewise important Caucasus classical antique carpet types, were rectilinear in design. This is also true of Persian carpets through the fifteenth-century Timurid period, as evidenced by Persian miniatures that include depictions of carpets presumably representing extant styles.

Toward the end of the fifteenth century and throughout the Safavid era, however, a new sort of carpet style developed, as is depicted in miniature paintings of the period and observable in surviving Safavid carpets, which date from the sixteenth century onward. The same new design inspiration appeared, although in a more naturalistic mode, in Mughal carpets of the same era. (The Mughals were the descendants of the Persianized Mongols who had ruled in Iran but, with the rise of Safavid power, had been obliged to move eastward, establishing their empire in India.)

The new design style in Persian carpets was the use of curvilinear floral motifs and the emergence of patterns that featured central medallions.[12] These carpets were developed with royal patronage and presumably involved the transfer of design elements and patterns used by manuscript illuminators to the medium of carpets. The new floral medallion carpets did not supplant the existing geometric carpets with their overall repeat patterns. Rather, both traditions of Persian carpet production continue to the present day.

By the seventeenth century, Persian pile carpets were in demand in Europe. Except for the distinctively yellow floral carpets called Polonaise carpets and a few other sorts, however, the carpets that got to Europe were not specifically produced for export. Commercial export production did not begin till the late 1800s. Rather, these carpets, most of them tribal, were generally made for the use of their producers and represented a sort of rural or tribal wealth and savings that went on the market in times of economic emergency when tribal families were forced to liquidate household goods.[13]

In the eighteenth century, carpets continued to be produced at the great centers of Tabriz, Kāshān, Esfahān, Kermān, and Herāt, as well as elsewhere. But eastern production in and around

---

11. Bennett, ed., *Complete Illustrated Rugs and Carpets of the World*, pp. 95–111, discusses and illustrates Holbein, Lotto, and Ushāk carpets, and, pp. 204–208, Transylvanian rugs under the heading "Bergama Rugs." Kurt Erdmann, *Seven Hundred Years of Oriental Carpets*, devotes separate chapters to Holbein and Lotto carpets. John Mills, "'Lotto' Carpets in Western Paintings," *Hali* 3 (1981): 278–289, is an interesting treatment. Sarah B. Sherrill, "Oriental Carpets in Seventeenth- and Eighteenth-Century America," *Antiques* 109 (January–June 1976): 142–167, features color plates of Holbein carpets in paintings, a Lotto design carpet, Transylvanian double-arch design carpets, and a Star Ushāk design carpet.

12. According to Dimand, *Oriental Rugs in the Metropolitan Museum of Art*, p. 37: "Judging from the representations of rugs in miniatures painted from the end of the fifteenth century, chiefly by the celebrated Behzād and his pupil Qāsem 'Ali, a great change in rug design took place at that time. The traditional geometric rugs still appear but they are outnumbered by rugs with arabesques and floral patterns, some with central medallions or with circular rather than angular compartments, formed by the intersecting circles or wavy lines and rendered in contrasting colors."

13. Robert Dillon, "Carpet Capitalism and Craft Involution in Kermān" (Ph.D. dissertation, Columbia University, 1976), p. 284.

Herāt suffered, owing to the Afghān invasions. Herāt itself, now the most important city in western Afghanistan, was lost to Iran after the brief mid-eighteenth-century reign of Nāder Shāh. Because of political turmoil and economic decline, many of the large manufactures throughout Iran became much less productive. More important, workshops formerly connected with the royal court all but disappeared. Thus weaving on a large scale was nonexistent for over a century, that is, from the end of the Safavid dynasty in the third decade of the eighteenth century till the latter part of the nineteenth century, when merchants, and not the royal court as had previously been the case, were responsible for a great expansion of the craft.

By the 1860s, Western influence began to be felt in the carpet industry. Western merchants organized aspects of the industry even to the point of deciding upon or providing designs and sometimes the materials for village weavers.[14] Two carpet types presumably influenced by the West are those with the popular Kermān floral medallion with a plain field in muted colors (see Fig. 9) and those with the Arāk medallion and atypically naturalistic flowers (see Fig. 10). These latter have a greater width than the traditional *miyān farsh*, or large central carpet in a room setting. At about this time, aniline dyes were discovered in England, and by the 1870s these synthetic dyes were being used on carpet wool all over the world, including Iran. By the 1870s Western scholarship on the subject of oriental carpets had begun.[15]

Also important for the future of Persian carpets, shipping routes opened up at this time on the Caspian Sea to the north, and maritime trade in the Persian Gulf greatly increased. A trade route through Turkey also was opened. In 1872, the Iranian monarch Nāseroddin Shāh granted a concession to a Baron de Reuter to build railways, irrigation works, and the like throughout Iran. In 1890 he granted a tobacco monopoly to a Major Talbot. Both concessions had to be withdrawn because of foreign pressure and because of local resistance to the agreements, a sign of growing consciousness among segments of the population as to their own national interests and rights.

In 1891, Iran sent a selection of carpets for display at the great Vienna World Exhibition. The continuing widespread Western fascination with oriental carpets can be dated from this occasion. Serious European and American commercial interest in Persian carpets ensued. Influence on Iranian carpet production from abroad became increasingly extensive, especially in the post–World War II period, and continued into the 1970s. In 1978, over 2.5 million square feet of new oriental rugs from Iran were imported into the United States alone.

Provenance

Perhaps the most discussed classification system for oriental rugs in general and Persian carpets in particular is that of provenance, which is to say the place where a carpet was woven. In the case of antique carpets, determination of carpet provenance is obviously important as an essential part of the establishment of the history of developments in oriental carpet-weaving. In the case of contemporary carpets, it is important in very practical terms. For the investor or buyer interested in carpets as furniture, the difference in cost between, for example, Kermān floral medallion with plain field design carpets woven in Romania, Iran, and India/Pakistan is considerable.

Another aspect of the importance of knowing in what city, town, or village or by what tribal group a particular Persian carpet has been produced is the information the carpet may provide about life in that locale. For example, carpets may lead to insights into the nature and traditions of crafts there or local attitudes toward the environment. Facts about the local economy, social structure, domestic architecture, and interior decoration might also be discerned in specific sorts of investigation of carpets from particular locales. Even if a particular carpet is obviously produced for export from its place of production, it may still offer such insights, as well as facts about local attitudes toward the world for which the carpet is intended beyond the place of origin.

In looking at the classification of carpets produced in Iran according to the geographical district or area in which carpets are produced *vis-à-vis* the range of designs embodied in Iranian carpets, one immediately sees the already cited basic distinction between curvilinear or floral and rectilinear or apparently geometric designs. It is also

---

14. Arthur Cecil Edwards, *The Persian Carpet*, pp. 55–56, describes Iranian commercial export production of Persian carpets in the nineteenth century.

15. David Sylvester, "On Western Attitudes to Eastern Carpets," in *Islamic Carpets from the Joseph V. McMullan Collection*, pp. 4–19, reviews nineteenth-century Western carpet scholarship, collector interest, and museum exhibitions.

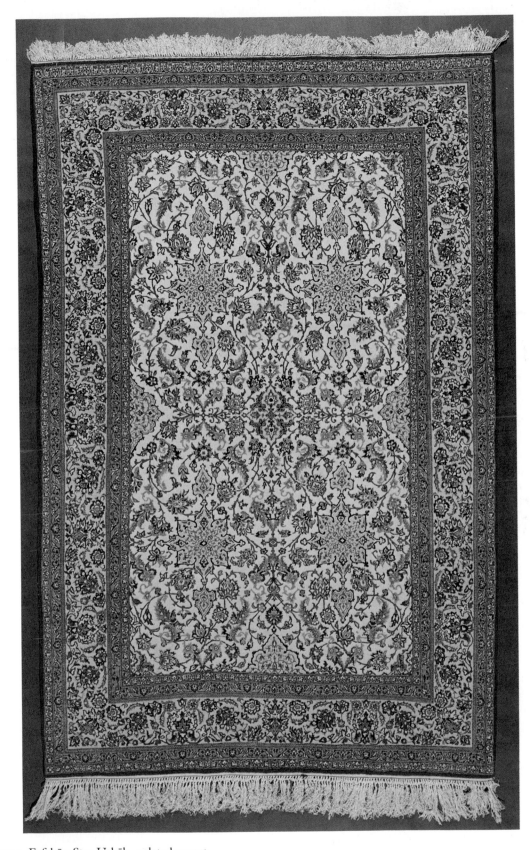

Figure 5. Esfahān Star Ushāk—related carpet.

evident that there is a relationship between city production—or village and town products commissioned or influenced by urban customers—and curvilinear designs, and between tribal production—or village or town production by weavers formerly associated with tribal groups—and rectilinear designs. Where city production involves rectilinear designs, the industry has derived its inspiration from a tribal or formerly tribal group, as in the cases of the Qom version of the Bakhtiyāri garden compartment carpet (see Fig. 23), Ardabil and Meshkinshahr carpets of Caucasus inspiration (see Fig. 20), and citified Ābādeh versions of Qashqā'i carpet types. There is something, therefore, to be said for categorizing contemporary Persian carpets as city and tribal. The latter term refers to any carpet made in Iran that exhibits methods of construction, motifs, and designs originating in nomad groups, regardless of whether or not the particular tribal group currently lives in Iran, has become sedentary, or still practices the craft of carpet-weaving. Conversely, a city carpet may be woven in the smallest of villages so long as it exhibits the basic methods, floral motifs, and curvilinear designs and patterns associated with city carpets. A third term, "village," might be used to refer to types that have hybrid designs, that is, designs that exhibit both tribal and urban inspiration and influences. Many Heris, Hamadān, and Varāmin carpets are examples.

The major carpet-weaving areas in Iran are generally referred to by the names of the major cities that serve as marketing hubs for carpets produced in outlying areas as well as for carpets produced in the cities themselves. These city-district areas are Tehrān, Qom, Kāshān, Kermān, Esfahān, Shirāz, Sanandaj, Hamadān, Arāk, Tabriz, Ardabil, Gorgān–Gonbad-e Qābus, Mashhad, and Yazd-Nā'in. But these designations do not immediately call to mind such important types of tribal carpets as Afshār, Bakhtiyāri, Baluch, Kurdish, Lor, Qashqā'i/Khamseh, and Yalameh. In each case, an urban marketing center is associated with the particular sort of tribal carpet. Baluch carpets are associated with Mashhad, Kurdish carpets with Sanandaj, Afshār carpets with Kermān, Bakhtiyāri and Lor carpets with Esfahān, and Qashqā'i/Khamseh and Yalameh carpets with Shirāz. In addition, as a result of the gradual settling of major Iranian tribal groups, much tribal carpet production takes place in urban centers or satellite villages where families have moved in order that the head of the household might find employment, while the women in the family there continue to weave carpets.

An inclusive geographical classification of Persian carpets that can give a feel for the extent of carpet-weaving in Iran is a region-by-region survey. There are at least ten more or less discrete regions reflecting important Persian carpet-producing centers and people.

First is the Caspian littoral, consisting of Gilān and Māzandarān provinces. In the eastern lowlands, around the city of Gorgān extending eastward to Gonbad-e Qābus, the bulk of Iranian Torkaman weaving is done. Otherwise, the Caspian region is one of the least significant areas of Iran in terms of pile carpet-weaving.

Second is the eastern region of Khorāsān. Its chief city is Mashhad, which is an active city carpet production and marketing center. Weaving is done in villages and towns all around Mashhad, as well as in Birjand, a city of over twenty-five thousand inhabitants located about halfway between Mashhad and Zāhedān. Weaving is also carried out in the region southwest of Mashhad and west of Birjand toward the desert in such towns as Ferdows and Tabas on the road to Yazd. The bulk of Baluch weaving is done in towns and villages throughout Khorāsān.

Third is the southeastern area of Baluchestān and Sistān. Some Baluch-inspired weaving is done in Zābol, a town of some twenty thousand people situated on a side road over one hundred miles northeast of Zāhedān, the main city in the region.

A fourth important carpet-weaving region is in Kermān province due west of Baluchestān and Sistān, extending from the major city of Kermān southward toward the Persian Gulf. The city of Kermān is one of the great names in Persian carpet-weaving and is in addition a marketing center for the region's tribal carpets, chief among them the products of the Afshārs.

A fifth region is the south-central area of Fārs. Its chief city, Shirāz, has a population of over 500,000 and is a marketing center for carpet-weaving done throughout the whole province, which extends southward toward the Persian Gulf. Its most famous carpets are Qashqā'i/Khamseh, Lor, and Yalameh goods, as well as the Qashqā'i-inspired "city" carpets woven in Ābādeh, a town of over 10,000 people north of Shirāz on the main road to Esfahān.

Sixth is the Persian Gulf region called Khuzestān. Its principal cities of Ahvāz and Ābādān may be familiar to Westerners. The region is not very important as a production area for *qāli* pile carpets.

The Esfahān region is a seventh area. It includes city weaving inspired by Esfahān itself in Nā'in, a town of fifteen thousand inhabitants one hundred miles to the northeast, and Najafābād, with a population of over eighty thousand, to the west. Josheqān, Maymeh, and the important weaving center of Kāshān to the north are likewise part of the Esfahān region. So are the tribal and village groups of Bakhtiyāri, Lor, and Boyer Ahmadi peoples to the west and southwest.

Eighth is the Tehrān region. Iran's capital city of over five million people is, of course, the most important oriental carpet marketing center in the world. Considerable weaving is also carried out in Tehrān. The important weaving locales in the region include the town of Varāmin, famous for a Kurdish-inspired carpet design, and the city of Qom, Iran's religious center located ninety miles south of the capital on the main road to Esfahān. Distinctive weaving is done also in Qazvin, a city of about 150,000 people, two hours by car west of the capital on the main road to Tabriz. The important weaving areas in and around Hamadān and Arāk can likewise be considered part of this region, if not a separate region in their own right.

To the west of the important carpet-producing region of Hamadān and influencing it is a ninth important area, the Kurdish region. Its largest city is Kermānshāh (renamed Bākhtarān in 1980) with a population of over 300,000. But the area's carpet weaving is traditionally more associated with the town of Bijār with a population of more than 10,000 and the city of Sanandaj, which has a population of over 100,000.

The tenth Iranian carpet-producing region is one of the most important. It is centered in the provinces of East and West Āzarbāyjān and is the major Turkish-speaking area in Iran. It extends from west of Qazvin on the Tehrān-Tabriz road and Āstārā by the Caspian westward to the Turkish and northward to the Russian border. There is Caucasus-inspired weaving at Ardabil and Meshkinshahr, as well as distinctive medallion designs from Heris and nearby Sarāb. The region's major city, Tabriz, is famous for a variety of Persian carpet types. In addition, distinctive carpets are woven in many other communities in the area, among them Ahar (population 40,000), Marand (population 40,000), and Zanjān (population 110,000).

As this brief sketch of weaving locales in Iran and any map of carpet-weaving areas imply, no other country associated with oriental carpet-weaving has such widespread weaving as Iran. Basically, the whole of Iran except for the Caspian littoral and the Persian Gulf region is involved in *qāli* carpet-weaving, marketing, and use.

Subject Matter

Except for some rectilinear patterns, chief among them most Torkaman designs and some Caucasus-inspired designs woven in Ardabil and Meshkinshahr, Persian carpet designs generally feature representational motifs.

One group depicts elements from identifiable historical monuments and Islamic buildings. One example is the interior dome design of Esfahān's Shaykh Lotfollāh Mosque depicted on Tabriz carpets. Also occasionally represented in Tabriz carpets is a ceiling pattern from the Safavid royal pavilion called Āli Qāpu also on the great Shāh Square in Esfahān. On some smaller carpets of Torkaman provenance, the famous tower after which the town Gonbad-e Qābus is named is represented. Or, as in the case of smaller carpets from Zābol, imaginary mosque domes are depicted to effect an arch shape at the top of the field, which is sometimes two-tiered.

Another subject depicted in smaller carpets to effect this arch shape is the *mehrāb*, the arch or alcove shape built into the wall of a mosque that faces Mecca, the direction Moslems face in their daily ritual prayers. (See Fig. 8.) Sometimes actual *mehrāb*s are represented in carpet designs, as in the case of some Esfahān carpets that feature the spandrels from a stucco *mehrāb* in Esfahān's Jāme' Mosque.

Of course, in defining the subject matter of particular Persian carpets by the names of the architectural decoration that inspires them, one still is at least one remove from saying exactly what the subject matter is. In other words, one needs to describe the subject matter on a wall, ceiling, or other surface adapted in a carpet design.

Perhaps the most familiar motif to appear in architectural decoration and Persian carpet designs is the arabesque. It appears, for example, on the exterior dome of the Shāh Mosque in Esfahān and in the spandrels of the Oljaytu *mehrāb* in the Jāme' Mosque. The word for "arabesque" in Persian is *eslimi*, which aptly emphasizes the association of the motif with Islam. The arabesque is a bifurcated shape extending out from a curving stem. (See Fig. 13.) "The arabesque was born from the idea of a leafy stem, but just as branches turn into unreal waves and spirals, so do leaves furcate and split into forms that do not occur in nature."[16]

Another extremely common motif that appears in the same sorts of Iranian Islamic architectural decoration and Persian carpets is called the *shāh 'abbāsi* motif. (See Fig. 6.) Named after Shāh 'Abbās the Great, the Safavid monarch who ruled from 1587 to 1629, the term refers to various complicated one-directional and stylized floral shapes that appear in the fields of many curvilinear carpet designs, among them common patterns woven in Kāshān and Esfahān.[17]

The *herāti* and *minā khāni* motifs are two related stylized floral motifs that are both traditional and popular in Persian carpets today. The word *herāti* means "of/relating to Herāt," the important city in western Afghanistan. Herāt is the site of an ancient city founded by Alexander the Great in 328 BCE. It was on the great Silk Route during the Middle Ages and became the capital of the Timurid empire under the reign of Shāhrokh (ruled 1405–1447). During the first half of the fifteenth century, Herāt was the most important cultural center in the region. Then in the sixteenth century it became a major urban center of the Safavid empire and a major carpet-producing region as well. In 1857 Herāt became part of Afghanistan, although it remains culturally Persian. Because of its historical connections with Persian empires and culture, it is natural for an almost ubiquitous Persian carpet motif to have the name *herāti*. The motif itself is a composite form. At its center is a symmetrical flower. Surrounding the flower are four identical, symmetrically placed leaf shapes. Between the leaves and the flower often appears a diamond shape that presumably represents a floral stem or stalk. The *herāti* motif appears in carpets woven all over Iran, from Kurdish products in the far west to Birjand carpets in the easternmost region. Many Hamadān area carpets feature *herāti* motifs.[18] (See Figs. 16, 17.)

The *minā khāni* motif is quite similar in or-

ganization to the *herāti* motif. It features a symmetrical flower around which four smaller, likewise symmetrical floral shapes are placed. Sometimes these four flowers are linked with a circular line that can be supposed as a stem or vine. As for the name *minā khāni*, its origin and meaning are not clear. By itself the Persian word *minā* can mean "daisy," which some *minā khāni* floral motifs resemble. In any case, it seems to have derived from the *herāti* motif. Both the *herāti* and *minā khāni* motifs, in turn, seem to relate to classical vase carpet floral motifs and their groupings. The *minā khāni* motif today is most associated with a carpet type woven in Varāmin.[19] (See Fig. 18.)

A more stylized, yet still demonstrably floral, motif is called *boteh* in Persian. Very simply, it is what is known in the West as the paisley or teardrop shape and appears in a wide variety of carpet designs woven all over Iran, for example, in carpets of Afshār, Arāk, and Qashqā'i provenance. (See Figs. 7, 34.) The word *boteh* in Persian means "shrubbery" or "clump of bushes." The characteristic division of shapes within the *boteh* shape seems to represent the complexity that a clump of bushes might have; the curved tip of the *boteh* motif may represent the movement of a bush or a shrub in the wind.

There are many other common motifs more easily identified. Trees of various sorts, among them cypress and weeping willow, appear as a dominant motif in some Lor, Baluch, Zābol, and other carpet types. Vase motifs with flower bouquets appear in various sorts of carpets including common designs from Qom and Rāvar. Almost realistic flowers appear as motifs in various curvilinear carpets, among them popular floral patterns woven in Arāk and Kermān. In the case of Bakhtiyāri, Qom, and Yalameh garden compartment carpets and garden scene carpets woven in Esfahān, Nā'in, Qom, Tabriz, and elsewhere, the garden scene subject matter determines the pattern. In such designs, there is a great variety of more or less stylized, but easily recognizable floral and tree shapes. Also in such designs as well as in other types of Baluch, Ardabil/Meshkinshahr, and Qashqā'i/Khamseh carpets, animal figures are depicted. Human figures appear as well in a popular hunting scene carpet type and in figure or portrait carpets mostly from Tabriz.

Besides the many Persian carpet motifs identi-

16. Ernst Kühnel, *The Arabesque: Meaning and Transformation of an Ornament*, p. 5.

17. Edwards, *The Persian Carpet*, pp. 43ff, presents illustrations of the variety of *shāh 'abbasi* motifs.

18. P. R. J. Ford, *The Oriental Carpet*, pp. 64–105, discusses the *herāti* motif in detail and includes illustrations of carpets exhibiting it of Kurdish (e.g., Bijār and Sanandaj), Farāhān, Hamadān, Malāyer, Qom, Tabriz, Tafresh, Varāmin, Yazd, and Zanjān provenance.

19. Edwards, *The Persian Carpet*, pp. 42–43, illustrates and briefly discusses the *minā khāni* motif.

Figure 6. *Shāh ʾabbāsi* motif (left). This Iranian stamp was issued in March 1975 to commemorate *(ayd-e) noruz*, the Iranian new year (festival) which begins on the first day of spring each year. The stamp features a typical example of the stylized floral motif named after Safavid Shāh ʾAbbās the Great (ruled 1587–1629). *Shāh ʾabbāsi* motifs, which are one-directional but symmetrical on the vertical axis, appeared in manuscript illumination, architectural decoration, and the like long before the reign of Shāh ʾAbbās, but because he was so famous for the sponsorship of great architectural monuments and other decoration featuring such motifs, they are known in Iran today by his name. It is significant to the appreciation of modern Persian carpets that an example of such a motif would be chosen for a stamp commemorating the coming of spring.

Figure 7. *Boteh* motif (right). This Iranian stamp, like that illustrated in Figure 6, was issued in March 1975 to commemorate the Iranian new year, which begins on the first day of spring each year. The stamp features two *boteh*s, stylized representations of a bush or shrubbery familiar in the West as a paisley or teardrop motif. *Boteh* motifs are almost ubiquitous in Iranian design, including various Persian carpet patterns, among them an overall *boteh* repeat design woven in the Arāk area and a Qashqāʾi medallion design illustrated in Figure 34.

fiable as deriving from nature, mostly floral, leaf, and vine shapes, there are more stylized motifs that seem geometric. Various sorts of medallion motifs, such as those that are characteristic of Ardabil/Meshkinshahr, Karājeh, Afshār, and Yalameh carpets, are difficult to appreciate as stylized flowers. The same is sometimes true of central medallions in Hamadān and Heris carpets.

The characteristic Torkaman motifs that appear in Torkaman, Baluch, and Zābol carpet types are the most apparently geometric motifs that appear in Persian carpets. These bi-axially symmetrical polygonal, mostly octagonal shapes are called *gol* in Persian. (See Figs. 11, 12.) The word *gol* can mean either "flower" in general or "rose." If in fact the Torkaman *gol* can be shown to be a stylized flower, then there is a case for arguing that from the most naturalistic to the most "geometric" motif in Persian carpets, the subject matter seems almost always to be floral.

Design

The classification of Persian carpets according to subject matter draws attention to their visual vocabulary. That vocabulary has been shown to be predominantly floral, whether motifs seem at first glance to be naturalistic, stylized, or geometric. The next step in classification is to consider carpets in terms of their design, that is, the composition created by the visual vocabulary of motifs.

In some cases, the subject matter is itself the pattern. Garden compartment carpets, such as those of Qom, Bakhtiyāri, and Yalameh provenance, are one obvious example. (See Figs. 21, 22, 23.) The same holds for figure or portrait carpets (see Fig. 24), prayer carpets featuring a *mehrāb* shape in the upper field area (see Fig. 8), vase and flowering shrub carpets, garden scene carpets (see Fig. 25), and hunting scene carpets (see Fig. 28).

Each of these very common contemporary patterns is typical of Persian carpet designs in general in being extremely conservative and traditional. In other words, each of the above patterns derives from classical antique Persian carpets that still serve as the models for modern carpets. For example, the 2,500-year-old Pazyryk carpet, with its field pattern of twenty-four compartments surrounding stylized flowers, is a prototype of sorts for modern compartment carpets that are direct descendants of formal garden designs from the fifteenth and sixteenth centuries. Actually, the Pazyryk carpet design itself is woven in Tehrān today. But the modern Tehrān versions are basically novelty items rather than a carpet design many Iranians would be comfortable using as a floorcovering. One interesting difference between the treatment of the floral motifs in the Pazyryk carpet's compartments and the standard representation of motifs in almost all Persian carpets from the sixteenth century onward is that no transition lines are drawn around the Pazyryk carpet's field quatrefoils; they are juxtaposed to the field color, whereas the standard practice in Persian carpets of whatever era and provenance is to bound every figure and motif with a transition line or another color to highlight the shape in contrast with another figure or the field color next to it.

To recognize that a particular carpet's design is determined by its identifiable subject matter or to appreciate a modern hunting, figure and portrait, or compartment pattern as being a version of a specific classical antique carpet is, however, different from classifying a carpet's pattern according to how its design elements are organized. This latter sort of classification is a key to identifying modern Persian carpets and to appreciating them as reflections of the society which produces them and in which they are so important as furniture.

Five basic kinds of patterns found in modern Persian carpets are (1) single-direction designs involving recognizable scenes from nature or animal and human figures; (2) prayer carpet designs that are likewise one-directional owing to the representation of the *mehrāb* arch at the upper end of the field area; (3) compartment or panel arrangements in the field area that may also be one-directional if tree motifs or bouquets of flowers appear in the compartments; (4) the many patterns that feature one or more medallions centrally placed on the vertical axis in the field, whose overall design may be one-directional, two-directional, or multidirectional depending upon the nature of the design elements used around the medallion(s); and (5) patterns achieved through the regular repetition of one or more motifs throughout the carpet field area, usually to effect a multidirectional design.

That a particular pattern is one-directional, two-directional, or multidirectional is obviously significant in furniture terms insofar as it is presumably inappropriate for persons in a given room to be obliged to observe a particular carpet design upside down. This concern is not unrelated to a basic design principle of many Persian carpet patterns: biaxial symmetry.

Biaxial symmetry means that a carpet's design is symmetrical on both vertical and horizontal axes. In other words, each quadrant or quarter of the carpet's surface is a mirror image of the other three quarters. The bottom left quarter, including field and border decoration, is mirrored by the bottom right quarter. The bottom right is mirrored by the upper right. If the upper right quarter is, as it were, flipped over, it becomes the upper left, which when turned over toward the bottom becomes the bottom left quarter. Biaxial symmetry is observable in many popular medallion and overall repeat designs of Afshār, Arāk, Esfahān, Hamadān, Heris, Joshe-qān, Kāshān, Kermān, Mashhad, Tabriz, Torkaman, Varāmin, and other provenance.

Biaxially symmetrical designs that do not include tree and animal motifs are generally multi-

Figure 8. A *mehrāb* in Esfahān's Jāme' Mosque. Issued in June 1980 by the Islamic Republic of Iran, this stamp commemorates the 1,400th anniversary of the hejira, the flight of the Moslem prophet Mohammad and his followers from Mecca to Medina. This event, which took place in 622 CE, marks the beginning of year one in the Moslem lunar calendar (A.H. = *anno hejirae*), in which, for example, 1985 corresponds with 1005/1006 A.H.

The stamp depicts part of the fourteenth-century Oljaytu Chamber of the Jāme' Mosque in Esfahān, specifically the *manbar* or pulpit in the center and the *mehrāb* or arched alcove or indentation to the right. (*Mehrāb*s, which are constructed in the wall of a mosque that faces Mecca, the direction toward which Moslems face in performing daily ritual prayers, are the essential motif in prayer carpets, such as those in Figures 25, 26, and 36.) The *mehrāb* illustrated in this stamp is made of stucco and has trefoils across the top horizontal band and arabesques in the spandrels. Similar trefoils and arabesques, as well as the spandrel shapes, are replicated in many prayer carpets.

directional. Those that do are generally two-directional; the top half of the pattern mirrors the bottom half, which means that animal figures that are right side up in the bottom half will appear upside down in the top half. In one-directional designs, there is often axial symmetry, which is to say that the left half of the field mirrors the right half. However, there are also one-directional garden scene and figure/portrait designs that lack any sort of symmetry.

The principle of biaxial symmetry means that in terms of furniture such carpet designs have the same appearance from wherever they are viewed in a room. This is an obvious advantage in their combined function as art and furniture. In a carpet whose design promises biaxial symmetry, that design is certainly flawed if, for example, a motif that appears in the upper left quadrant does not appear in a comparable place in the other three quadrants.

Those Persian carpets whose subject matter is their design, such as prayer carpets, hunting carpets, figure/portrait carpets, and the like are easily identified and classified in terms of pattern. But it is not as easy at the outset to discern the nature of the pattern in many multidirectional carpets, which appear to exhibit a "multiplicity of individual carpet designs." In fact, most traditional patterns are permutations and combinations of a handful or so of pattern ideas and combinations of components. In one scholar's view, "the apparent multiplicity of individual carpet design in fact represents variants and combinations of . . . four basic compositions." These are "compartment," "trellis," "medallion," and "tendril" compositions that "frequently consist of an integration of several 'layers' of design."[20] The most common of these is the medallion design.

Medallion designs in the field can be of five basic sorts: (1) one essentially symmetrical figure in the center; (2) one essentially symmetrical figure in the center, with the corners usually drawn from similar elements; (3) either (1) or (2) with vertically arranged pendants; (4) symmetrical figures the length of the vertical axis; and (5) one medallion or several in a series arranged at intervals across the field. The parts of the field not covered with medallion elements make use of patterns and motifs such as the repeating forms.

There are a large number of more or less stylized floral and vegetal forms, simple and composite, that can be repeated to create the design of a Persian carpet field area. They and alternating transitional motifs may be the sole decoration in the field area. Or they may be a sort of background to medallions, single or multiple, with or without pendants on the vertical axis, and with or without corner elements. Chief among these repeating forms are the *herāti* motif, the *minā khāni* motif, the *boteh* figure, the *gol-e hennā* [henna flower] motif, the various Torkaman *gol* motifs, the various *shāh 'abbāsi* motif shapes, and arabesque with vine combinations.

Somewhat between the repeating forms and medallion designs in conception are the panel or compartment arrangements found in Bakhtiyāri garden compartment carpets, citified versions of them woven in Qom, simple versions in natural wool colors woven in Tabriz and elsewhere, and the distinctive Yalameh compartment carpets with geometric, Caucasus-inspired medallion shapes within the compartments. In carpets of this sort, the field is divided into square, lozenge, or rectangular areas each containing a single design motif or combination. *Boteh*s, weeping willow trees, cypress trees, bunches of flowers, vases

with flowers, and *shāh 'abbāsi* motifs are examples.

The composition of the borders of Persian carpets is another telling aspect of design, but there is more similarity among the major types of carpets in border design than in field design. There are basically three kinds of border: the main border, which usually embodies the repetition of one or more, often complex, floral or geometric devices; the subsidiary or secondary border, usually comprised of relatively simple elements such as vine figures and leaves or elements such as the reciprocal trefoil; and border stripes. The main border is usually wider than the subsidiary borders, which are normally paired about the main border. Prominent border motifs include calligraphy, often stylized in the early Arabic script called Kufic; pseudo-calligraphy; serrated leaf and flower calyx combination; what is popularly called the hour-glass motif in conjunction with some other repeated motif; the *shāh 'abbāsi* motif; other palmettes; the Torkaman line; stars such as the eight-pointed star; what is popularly termed the running dog pattern; latch-hooks; and the like.

In design terms, the main border has a two fold function. First, it generally complements in color or shapes something about the field pattern, which will invite the observer to look again at the field of the carpet. Second, it has its own motion around the whole rectangle of the carpet. In other words, main borders are usually designed as continuous through alternation of shapes and linking elements. The alternation may be of motifs small and large with respect to each other, dark and light, inverted, or repeated elements joined together with a line that proceeds around the whole carpet. The only way exact regularity and continuity of the border can be assured all the way around the carpet is for a cartoon to be used in the weaving. This is the case in curvilinear designs, where any irregularity in the border as it approaches corners renders the carpet less valuable in market and aesthetic terms. However, in the case of rectilinear designs that are woven from memory, very often only the corner of the main border area where the weaving begins will be exact in terms of the placement and movement of border motifs. For example, if the weaving starts at the lower right, there may be noticeable irregularities at the lower left and both upper corners insofar as the weaver may not be able to anticipate exactly where and when a corner needs to be begun *vis-à-vis* completion of field motifs and pattern. Almost all of the tribal

20. Hanna Erdmann, "Zür Formenwelt des Orient-teppichs," *Hali* 1 (1978): 339–344.

carpets illustrated later in this volume exhibit these irregularities. They are not counted as flaws in the marketplace. Whether they represent flaws in aesthetic terms is another matter. In any case, the popular view that such miscalculations are part of the charm of tribal weaving or are deliberately introduced by weavers hesitant to compete with Allāh by trying to do something perfectly[21] is a subjective response on the part of observers. A final note: the main borders of most carpets are wider on the lengthwise sides than they are across the top and bottom of the carpet.

A Checklist of Persian Carpet Types

There are scores of readily distinguishable types of Persian carpets on the market today. They are sold under names that refer to provenance, basic design elements, patterns, function, and materials.

The following checklist presents in alphabetical order the names of fifty-five very common types that the Persian carpet *amateur* should have little difficulty finding in oriental carpet stores that specialize in modern Persian carpets. Because most of the Persian carpet types listed below are described in the course of the book, readers should be able to identify most of them by sight. Most of the place names and names of tribal groups are shown on Maps 1 and 2. Italicized Persian terms are defined as they appear in discussions of individual Persian carpets. The index can be used to locate the definitions. For carpet types illustrated in this book, the figure number appears after the type name. For illustrations of types illustrated in this book, the figure number appears after the type name. For illustrations of types not depicted in this book, see the bibliography, in which Persian carpet types are cited by name under the titles and authors of book-length studies that include color plates.

Ābādeh Qashqā'i *boteh* medallion design carpet
Afshār multiple medallion carpet (Fig. 19)
Arāk (= Sāruq) medallion carpet (Fig. 10)
Arāk American floral medallion carpet
Arāk *boteh* field carpet
Ardabil/Meshkinshahr multiple medallion carpet (Fig. 20)
Ardabil/Meshkinshahr Lotto design carpet (Fig. 4)
Ardabil/Meshkinshahr Perepedil design carpet
Bakhtiyāri garden compartment carpet (Fig. 22)

Bakhtiyāri Esfahān-design medallion carpet
Baluch *gol* carpet
Baluch tree-of-life prayer carpet (Fig. 36)
Birjand medallion with *herāti* motif carpet
Esfahān arabesque medallion and floral field carpet (Fig. 13)
Esfahān garden scene prayer carpet (Fig. 25)
Fārs (= Khamseh/Qashqā'i or Lor) lion rug (Fig. 27)
Hamadān area medallion with *herāti* field carpet (Fig. 17)
Heris area medallion carpet (Fig. 14)
Josheqān diamond cluster field with medallion carpet (Fig. 15)
Kalārdasht multiple medallion carpet
Karājeh medallion repeat carpet
Karājeh multiple medallion carpet
Kāshān medallion carpet
Kāshān *afshān* field carpet (Fig. 33)
Kermān floral medallion with plain field carpet (Fig. 9)
Kurdish (= Bijār or Sanandaj) *herāti* field carpet
Lor tree-of-life field carpet
Marand natural wool color medallion carpet
Mashhad *lachak-toranj* design carpet (Fig. 35)
Mazlaqān medallion carpet with stepped polygonal field
Nā'in medallion with *shāh 'abbāsi* field carpet
Nā'in Star Ushāk design carpet
Qāsemābād *herāti* motif and bird carpet
Qashqā'i/Khamseh scarab medallion carpet
Qashqā'i *boteh* medallion with Persepolis columns carpet (Fig. 34)
Qashqā'i *gabeh* carpet
Qom silk medallion carpet
Qom Bakhtiyāri design garden compartment carpet (Fig. 23)
Qom *mehrābi*/gateway prayer carpet (Fig. 26)
Rāvar carpet
Tabriz Ardabil Shrine design carpet (Fig. 37)
Tabriz figure/portrait carpet
Tabriz garden scene carpet
Tabriz hunting scene carpet (Fig. 28)
Tabriz mosque-dome design carpet
Torkaman Salor *gol* carpet
Torkaman Tekkeh *gol* carpet (Fig. 11)
Torkaman Yomut *kepseh gol* carpet
Torkaman dome prayer carpet
Torkaman "geometric" motif prayer carpet
Varāmin *minā khāni* field carpet (Fig. 18)
Yalameh multiple medallion carpet
Yalameh garden compartment carpet (Fig. 21)
Zābol *gol* carpet (Fig. 12)
Zābol tree-of-life carpet

21. According to Bess Allen Donaldson, *The Wild Rue: A Study f Muhammadan Magic and Folklore in Iran* (London: Luzac, 1938), p. 19, deliberate flaws are woven into carpets to ward off the evil eye.

3. A Portfolio of Modern Persian Carpets

During the years between the mid-1950s and the late 1970s, literally hundreds of distinguishable types of handcrafted pile carpets could be found in Iranian carpet stores and homes. There were portrait carpets of Mohammad Rezā Pahlavi no bigger than 1' × 1' in size. At the other extreme, there was the monumental Esfahān carpet commissioned by the Shāh in 1975 for the Parliament Building in Tehrān, a square carpet 33' × 33' woven by about twenty-eight women working together. Some 3'6" × 5' Baluch carpets were selling at $30–40 apiece, while in late 1979 a nineteenth-century silk Tabriz carpet auctioned in Geneva for $817,000, a record to that date.[1] Contrasting with the simplest rectilinear and geometric designs, such as the distinctive multiple medallion patterns from the Kalārdasht region north of Tehrān, were the most obviously curvilinear and floral carpets featuring numerous sorts of medallion patterns from hundreds of villages, towns, and urban weaving centers. There were also the various overall repeat and compartment patterns, such as compartment designs of Qom and Yalameh carpets, natural-wool-colored versions of Bakhtiyāri designs woven in Tabriz, and various contemporary sorts of one-directional scene and prayer carpets.

With the establishment of the Islamic Republic of Iran in the spring of 1979 and subsequent diminution of Iranian trade and other relations with Western Europe and the United States, the quantity of Persian carpets exported to the West decreased markedly. Newer Persian carpets on the market in the early 1980s were mostly goods which had been warehoused earlier in Europe.

As for Persian carpet production itself, it dropped by the mid-1980s up to 50 percent in the case of more finely woven carpets, but perhaps increased somewhat in less finely woven carpet types. One Iranian art critic opines that the reason for this is that the larger entrepreneurs and major merchants are investing less confidently in weaving, a situation which leaves weavers, who may lack the wherewithal personally to finance more finely woven carpets, to strike off on their own.[2]

In any case, there seem to be no significant differences in design and types between carpets produced in the later Pahlavi years and those produced in Khomayni's Iran, that is, from the late 1950s into the 1980s. As a means of suggesting the range of contemporary Persian carpet types and familiarizing the reader with design possibilities, thirteen of the commonest and most distinctive designs are here described and analyzed.

Kermān Floral Medallion with Plain Field Carpet

Perhaps the best-known Persian carpet design and the one most associated with "Persian" as opposed to other oriental carpet-weaving traditions is a Kermān floral medallion design with floral pendants on the vertical axis. (See Fig. 9.) The medallion is what first attracts attention, but then the observer is struck by the expanse of rich, unbroken field color that competes with and balances the visual forcefulness of the medallion and pendant activity on the vertical axis. This Kermān design generally features corner floral elements that include motifs complementing the medallion shapes. The corner elements often move along the lengthwise inner borders up to the center of the field sides.

---

1. Aimée L. Morner, "Investments You Can Stand On," *Fortune* (January 12, 1981), p. 109.

2. Karim Emāmi, personal communication, July 31, 1983. Post-Pahlavi oriental carpet production and export levels are described by Laila Hemmat, "Iran's Carpet Slump," *Middle East* (December 1982), p. 54; R. E. G. Macey, "Filling the Persian Gap," *Hali* 2 (1980): 294–296; Rita Reif, "Rugs: Some Pieces Are Still Climbing," *New York Times* (April 6, 1980); "Iranian Carpet Output Declines," *Kayhan International* (March 15, 1978), p. 8; and *Iranshahr*, no. 184 (April 1, 1983): 5.

This design is what first comes to mind when one thinks of carpets from the Kermān area. Kermān is the most important east-central city of Iran and the capital of Kermān province. It has been an important textile production center since at least the establishment of the Safavid dynasty (1501–1722) and is one of the most important Persian carpet production areas today, with carpets exhibiting four or five distinct grades in terms of density of pile, that is, knot count. Like almost all Persian city carpets, Kermān carpets use cotton warps and wefts. Kermān carpets also feature pile that is distinctive in two respects. First, the wool is relatively soft. Second, the pile is not closely clipped. The relative deepness of the Kermān carpet pile helps effect the richness and sometimes subtle variations in the plain field color around the medallion area.

Although the Kermān floral medallion with plain field pattern is today a quintessential Iranian city carpet design, its original inspiration, unlike that of many modern tribal carpet designs, does not come from textile traditions and patterns. Rather, it traces its origin to the revolution in Persian carpet design that occurred during the Safavid era.

The Kermān design was the result of the adaptation by carpet designers of existing designs used in Timurid and Safavid manuscript illumination.[3] On decorated pages of manuscripts, the handwritten text was very often framed on the rectangular page by borders containing floral and other vegetal motifs not unlike the traditional floral forms represented in city carpet border designs. The manuscript covers, title pages, and colophon pages often featured a medallion shape in the center, perhaps with pendants on the vertical axis, and borders within which some corner elements might be drawn. The rest of the field area might be left in plain color without decoration.

This same origin is assumed for other curvilinear designs involving a central medallion with or without corner elements and with more or less decorative field activity around the medallion. Arāk (= Sāruq) medallion carpets, Esfahān arabesque medallion and field carpets, and various *lachak-toranj* [medallion with corner elements] carpets woven throughout Iran are other examples of common contemporary designs that owe their original inspiration to the Safavid royal court and the transfer from book to textile designers in the sixteenth century. In fact, almost all of the contemporary curvilinear Persian carpet types owe their inspiration to this practice.

On the other hand, the rectilinear designs of today are inheritors of Turkish traditions that date back at least to the Saljuq conquest of the Iranian plateau in the middle of the eleventh century. The Torkaman Tekkeh *gol* carpet is a modern Iranian example *par excellence* of the Turkic tradition. Some experts prefer the rectilinear designs precisely because they are allegedly "faithful to laws of textile manufacture," whereas Safavid and Safavid-inspired curvilinear designs are "products of decadence." Thus "the rug became just another medium through which the same basic themes and ideas that dominated painting, book illumination, and even architectural decoration of the Safavid period were expressed."[4]

The Kermān floral medallion with plain field design is often less than traditional even in post-Safavid Iranian terms for several reasons. First, the colors are less vivid, more muted, and more pastel than the more traditional color combinations of Iranian medallion carpets. Second, the relative squareness of the carpet (in contrast to the more traditional Iranian city carpet shape in which the length is nearly twice the width) is likewise a rather modern feature of the carpet. The influence of Western consumers, Americans in particular, led to these changes in color and shape. This influence began to be felt in Persian carpet production toward the end of the nineteenth century when European and American firms set up offices from which to organize carpet exportation to the West. These firms subsequently determined sizes, shapes, and colors in the case of many carpets produced for export.

Another noteworthy aspect of the popular Kermān floral medallion design is the expanse of field color, a major part of its appeal in the West. In comparison with other medallion patterns, the Kermān design is less busy and less intricate; it also exhibits fewer colors. Consequently, it would naturally fit better into a room environment in

---

3. This "corner and medallion" design is discussed and illustrated as deriving from fifteenth-century book covers by Arthur Cecil Edwards, *The Persian Carpet*, pp. 41–42.

4. Ernst J. Grube, "The Joseph V. McMullan Collection of Islamic Carpets," in *Islamic Carpets* (New York: Near Eastern Art Research Center, 1965), p. 10; Oktay Aslanapa, "Seljuk and Ottoman Carpets," in *Turkish Art and Architecture* (London: Faber and Faber, 1971), p. 299.

Figure 9. Kermān floral medallion with plain field carpet.

which the shapes and colors of other furniture compete for attention than would busier, more intricate patterns that seem appropriate in traditional Iranian room settings in which the carpet itself is the major piece of furniture. Until the recent past, most middle class urban Iranians usually ate on the floor, using cloths to cover the carpet, the design of which was enough to make the whole room alive, warm, and interesting. Although the Kermān design is perfectly suited to such a style of life, it may also be better, in terms of interior design, for more cluttered Western rooms than are busier curvilinear designs.

Arāk Medallion with Floral Field Carpet

Carpets woven in the Arāk area are also referred to as Sāruq carpets because Sāruq is the name of the valley in which the city of Arāk, some four hours southwest of Tehrān on the road from Qom to Hamadān, is located. Arāk or Sāruq carpets have been an important and popular sort of Iranian carpet in the West since the end of the nineteenth century. In fact, the first foreign carpet dealer to establish an office in Iran did so in Arāk, then known as Soltānābād, in 1883. From that time on, European and American firms purchased and manufactured carpets there for export. Actually, however, Arāk carpets had reached Western markets even before the 1880s as a result of their being shipped to Istanbul in the 1870s by Tabriz merchants.

One readily identifiable pattern associated with the names Arāk and Sāruq is an overall repeat pattern involving *boteh*s as the sole field motif. The *boteh* tips often alternate left and right; they are otherwise arranged in symmetrical ways to create a variety of effects on the field color which shows around them. An overall repeat pattern consisting exclusively of *boteh* motifs is also woven in Afshār tribal carpets. But the Arāk *boteh* pattern is obviously a city, rather than a tribal, sort of carpet because of its room-sized dimensions, the regularity of size and shape of its *boteh*s, its curvilinear border patterns, and its cotton warps and wefts.

A second popular Arāk/Sāruq carpet style is a floral medallion carpet with floral corner elements and perhaps other floral materials along the borders lengthwise down the field. (See Fig. 10.) Enough field color may show through to remind one of the Kermān floral medallion with plain field carpet, but the typical Arāk carpet has more activity in the field around the medallion than do Kermān carpets. Such floral activity in

Figure 10. Arāk medallion with floral field carpet.

Arāk medallion patterns can consist of traditional *shāh 'abbāsi* motifs, vines, tendrils, and leaves. This design is also typical of contemporary carpets woven throughout the area from Hamadān eastward to Arāk; these carpets appear on the market under the names Borchalu, Dargazin, Kabutrahang, Lilihān, Mahallāt, and Mehrebān, as well as Sāruq. Even though the carpet expert who knows wool, dyes, and weaving techniques can readily distinguish among the products of these various city, town, and village weaving areas, distinctions among the places in which such relatively similar carpets are woven are not made here with these carpets. In any case, the classical antique Farāhān, Malāyer, and Sāruq floral patterns from the Arāk area are often appreciated as being among the most aesthetically appealing Persian carpet types in history.

Arāk medallion carpets as well as Kermān medallion with plain field carpets often combine traditional central medallion and floral motifs with less stylized, more naturalistic flowers in sprays and bouquets that are not Safavid or even Iranian in origin. Carpets featuring such flowers

Figure 11. Torkaman Tekkeh *gol* carpet: detail.

and their patterning are often referred to as being in the "American style" because these flowers were introduced into carpet designs by American dealers whose clients preferred them to patterns with more traditional flowers. Since the 1920s, these American style Arāk and Kermān carpets have been in great abundance and are as popular in Iran as abroad. The fact of American influence on design elements of Arāk and Kermān carpets is viewed by some experts as a disastrous development; it is one of the circumstances of recent Persian carpet production that persuade many oriental carpet experts to think of most contemporary Iranian production as "corruption" of earlier great art.[5]

Another significant feature of the design of most Arāk and Kermān medallion carpets is biaxial symmetry, in which each quarter of a carpet is a mirror of the other quarters. (See Figs. 9, 10.)

Torkaman *Gol* Carpets

If the Kermān floral medallion with plain field carpet is a quintessential modern descendant of the curvilinear prototypes with patterns adapted from manuscript illumination, Torkaman *gol* carpets are equally classic modern descendants of an obviously different prototype of oriental carpet design. The most familiar Torkaman design is an overall repeat pattern involving an octagonal, rectilinear major motif alternating with a smaller motif of the same sort or a cruciform/stellate secondary motif. Modern Torkaman carpets produced in Iran are heir to the weaving traditions of the Turkish Saljuqs and Ottomans. Such traditions are represented in depictions of oriental carpets in European paintings from the fourteenth century onward. In the literature they are referred to as Holbein carpets, after Hans Holbein the Younger (1497[?]–1543), the most prominent of the painters in whose paintings such designs appeared.

Two such paintings are particularly famous. One is Holbein's own *The French Ambassadors at the English Court*, which hangs in the National Gallery in London. In part of the painting two ambassadors are standing on either side of a high table over which is draped a rectilinear carpet with a red field, parts of two octagonal *gol* motifs visible on it.[6] The other much illustrated painting, on permanent display in London's National Portrait Gallery, is called *The Somerset House Conference*. It portrays two groups of men seated along the sides of a table on which is spread a bold red, blue, and black repeat pattern carpet. The pattern features as the major motif octagons similar to Torkaman motifs in carpets that have survived from the latter part of the eighteenth century onward.

Torkamans constitute the major group in Soviet Turkmenistan, east of the Caspian Sea; they are also a major part of the population in northern Afghanistan. In the northeastern region of Iran, Torkamans inhabit the area from the southeast corner of the Caspian littoral through Gorgān to Gonbad-e Qābus. Among the nine or so major tribal groups producing carpets in Iran today, the Torkamans are ethnically distinctive. They are a Mongol Turkic race and descendants of the Central Asian Oghuz Turks who migrated west-

5. P. R. J. Ford, *The Oriental Carpet*, pp. 280 ff., especially plate 636 and commentary.

6. Color plates of these much-illustrated paintings appear in Ford, *The Oriental Carpet*, and Fabio Formenton, *Oriental Rugs and Carpets*, trans. Pauline L. Phillips (New York: McGraw-Hill, 1970).

ward from Mongolia in the tenth century. They are also related to the Saljuqs who conquered the Iranian plateau region in the middle of the eleventh century and, after occupying the caliphal city of Baghdād, ruled Irān as part of an Islamic empire from 1053 to 1157.

Torkaman textile designs are likewise distinctive in comparison with the carpet-weaving traditions of other tribal groups in Iran. Torkaman pile carpet products are varied in function from tent bands, tent flap covers, horse and camel blankets, covers for containers and vessels of various sorts, and saddle bags, to small prayer carpets of various designs and other carpets of all sizes. In comparison with almost all other Iranian tribal rug types, most Torkaman carpets are relatively finely woven and closely clipped. Equally distinctive is the fact that their designs are almost exclusively overall repeat patterns featuring the rectilinear polygonal major motif called *gol* in Persian and often either a smaller *gol* or a cruciform/stellate shape as an alternated minor motif. Another distinctive feature of most Torkaman designs when compared with Afshār, Qashqā'i, and other Iranian tribal carpets is their regularity and exactness of motif placement. Designs are meant to be perfectly symmetrical. There is no place for floral scatter as in Afshār and Qashqā'i carpets. The individual Torkaman weaver is highly constrained in terms of spontaneity and creative freedom.

These facts do not imply a lack of either creativity on the part of weavers or variety in the design of contemporary Torkaman carpets woven in Iran. There are a dozen or more standard *gol* shapes, each with a traditional name indicating specific Torkaman tribes or clans whose weaving featured distinctive *gol* shapes. Although the names Chodor, Ersāri, Salor, Saryk, Tekkeh, and Yomut may not have great meaning in Iran today because Torkaman groups and patterns there have mingled, they serve adequately as designations for possible Torkaman *gol* types. Furthermore, Torkaman weaving traditions and their various *gol* motifs have been influential among non-Torkaman Iranians in whose communities the Torkamans have lived. There are palpable Torkaman influences in common carpets produced by Baluch nomads and villagers in Khorāsān and to the south and by the people in the Zābol area near Zāhedān in southeast Iran. One very common Zābol design features an overall repeat pattern of a Torkaman Tekkeh or Salor *gol* and an alternating secondary *gol* motif in orange,

crimson, green, and other bright colors not typically Torkaman. (See Fig. 12.)

As for the Torkaman *gol* motifs and patterns themselves, the Ersāri tribe gives its name to those distinctive coarsely woven Afghanistan carpets of various sizes that feature large squarish *gol*s outlined in black on a field which is usually dark red. In Iran, where these products of Afghanistan have long been readily available on the market, the typical Ersāri carpet is often referred to simply as an Afghān carpet; and the Ersāri *gol* motif is often called *pā fil* or "elephant's foot" in Persian.

Among Torkaman *gol* motifs and patterns commonly woven in Iran are the Salor, Yomut, and Tekkeh types.[7]

One Salor *gol* is more rounded than the Ersāri "elephant's foot" *gol* and appears in more finely woven carpets than does the latter. In general, except for the Ersāri carpets from Afghanistan, Torkaman carpets are the most finely woven among all oriental tribal carpets. Another Salor *gol* is also octagonal, but features tips that extend beyond the outer perimeter of the octagon; within it, instead of a quincunx plan, there is often a biaxially symmetrical figure with *gotshak* [ram's horns] motifs that are generally referred to as "double latch hooks" in the West.

Another important *gol* type found in contemporary Torkaman carpets from Iran is a Yomut *gol* that is basically diamond-shaped with "latch hooks" extending beyond the diamond perimeter creating a larger diamond figure whose circumference the observer imagines on the basis of the line implied by the flat outer edges of the latch hooks, which are all the same length. This *gol* is called *dyrnak* and usually appears in diagonal rows as a single repeated motif in the carpet field. A second Yomut *gol* is called *kepseh*, a word that means "sheaf" in Torkaman. The *kepseh gol* is likewise diamond-shaped and lacking an outer perimeter line; instead, above and below the horizontal axis, there are oblong shapes with serrated edges that decrease in height from the central point on the vertical axis to both ends on the horizontal axis. These *kepseh gol*s are repeated as the sole motif in the field pattern in alternating colors in diagonal rows.

---

7. Werner Loges, *Turkoman Tribal Rugs*, provides color plates of carpets featuring classic nineteenth-century Tekkeh, Salor, Saryk, Yomut, Chodor, Kizilayak, Ersāri, and Arabatshi gol *motifs*, accompanied by drawings of the different motifs.

A third Yomut *gol* is very similar to a common Saryk *gol*. Both are octagonal shapes that extend outward on the horizontal axis and are often linked one to another in a repeat pattern of rows across the carpet field.

A number of other Torkaman *gols* appear mostly in carpets woven in Afghanistan and Central Asia. They are much illustrated in the literature, and such great attention paid to Torkaman weaving in oriental carpet literature parallels the impression that more people in the West are interested in Torkaman carpets than in any other sort, city or tribal.[8]

Another word used to refer to these *gol* or stylized rose shapes is the Turkic word *gül*, which can mean both "rose" and, in the view of some scholars, "emblem" or "identifying insignia," a sort of coat of arms.[9] Accordingly, the distinctive *gols* of each Torkaman tribe are thought to have originally been those tribes' distinctive *güls* or insignia. Yomut *gols* are supposed to have stood for the Yomut people, the Sayrk for the Sayrk people, etc. Among Torkamans weaving carpets in Iran, however, there is no awareness of such significance to the different shapes of *gols*. Furthermore, many Torkamans are not aware of tribal distinctions and subgroups.

Besides the overall repeat patterns involving the alternation of *gols* and secondary motifs that may be *gols* or cruciform/stellate figures, Torkaman carpets in Iran also include various sorts of prayer carpet designs. One involves a rectangular indentation at the top of the field area which is covered with regularly shaped and placed rectilinear motifs that cannot be identified with certainty as floral in nature. A second popular type creates its one-directionality through the depiction of a dome in the upper half of the field rather than a replication of a *mehrāb* shape. In these prayer carpets, the characteristic Torkaman fineness of weave, close clipping of pile, and pre-

dominant use of red are almost always found. However, owing to the availability of good synthetic dyes throughout northeastern Iran, many modern Torkaman carpets on the market in Tehrān and abroad feature untraditional colors albeit always with traditional patterns.

The most common Torkaman design woven in Iran today is a Tekkeh *gol* pattern. (See Fig. 11.) This design type is called Tekkeh after the major Torkaman tribe of that name which, incidentally, was the last politically independent Torkaman tribal group, subjugated by the Czarist Russians in 1881. Among Torkaman groups in Iran, the Tekkeh and the Yomut are the most numerous.

The Tekkeh *gol* carpet usually features a red field covered with distinctive *gol* major motifs, each with four quadrants and a central square, and alternating cruciform or stellate secondary motifs. Many of these modern Torkaman designs also feature a main border of alternating shapes that appear to be suns, moons, or stars with rays emanating from their polygonal shapes.

Such Tekkeh *gol* carpets are among the most finely woven and closely clipped Persian tribal carpets. Part of their appeal is the clarity and definiteness of their rectilinear motifs and placement. Another distinctive reason for the appeal of the Tekkeh and other Torkaman *gol* carpets is their use of space. There is hardly a Persian carpet type, other than one popular pattern from the Rāvar village area near Kermān, that does not exhibit the firm presence of a field ground color behind the motifs and the pattern they form. (The Rāvar design in question, on the other hand, is an extremely busy floral medallion with floral field design through the motifs of which no field color shows.) According to one Persian carpet expert: "Expressive spacing is difficult, and among modern painters rare. But it is . . . fundamental to the rug weaver's craft even at the simplest . . . ; and in this particular perhaps no other art can teach so much."[10]

In the Tekkeh *gol* carpet, the field color combines with the regularly placed *gols* and secondary motifs woven from memory to create individual effects in individual carpets. The key to the individuality, in the face of distinctive Torkaman regularity of design, lies in the spacing effected by motifs that are not exactly like one another, that are individual because they are not mechanically woven from a cartoon.

8. "Editorial," *Hali* 2 (1980): 273–274, reported a survey conducted by the magazine that verifies the great contemporary interest in Torkaman carpets.

9. On the meaning of the term *gol*, the origin of Torkaman *gols*, and the issue of their alleged significance as a tribal emblem, there is much speculation. For the now traditional view that Torkaman *gols* are both flowers and tribal emblems, see Robert and Frances M. Pinner, *Turkoman Studies I* (Atlantic Highlands, N.J.: Humanities Press, 1980). Also of interest in this regard is Jon Thompson and Louise Mackie, eds., *Turkoman Tribal Carpets and Traditions* (Washington, D.C.: Textile Museum, 1980).

10. Eric Schroeder, "The Art of Looking at Rugs," in *McMullan Exhibition*, p. 12.

Figure 12. Zābol *gol* carpet.

Esfahān Arabesque Medallion and Field Carpet

One of the most distinctive medallion patterns woven in Iran today is a particularly popular Esfahān design. (See Fig. 13.) Part of its distinctiveness and special appeal has to do with the composition of floral material in the field.

Intertwined among the *shāh 'abbāsi* and other floral elements in the biaxially symmetrical field pattern are circular vines that terminate in bifurcating arabesque leaf shapes. One of the tips of each of these arabesques encircles an earlier section of the vine from which it proceeded. This design feature causes the eye to return to the vines and move elsewhere in viewing the carpet. In other words, a sense of endlessness or of a new possibility for observing the design presents

itself at every turn. This combination of a *shāh 'abbāsi* field and circular vines terminating in arabesques is distinctive of carpets from Esfahān, although the combination usually occurs in conjunction with other features of the carpet as described below. The design mirrors, albeit in different colors, the essence of the pattern produced in tile on the external surface of Esfahān's famous Shāh Mosque and is consequently associated with Esfahān, the country's most important tourist center during the 1960s and 1970s.

The Shāh Mosque was commissioned in 1612 by Safavid Shāh 'Abbās the Great, who ruled from 1587 to 1629. It was one of numerous great projects of construction commissioned by Shāh 'Abbās in Esfahān and elsewhere. He was responsible for the building of the shrine to Emām Rezā's sister Ma'sumeh Fātemeh in Qom as well as for some construction at the Emām Rezā Shrine precincts in Mashhad to which he had once made a pilgrimage from Esfahān on foot.

In 1598, Shāh 'Abbās had moved the Iranian capital from Qazvin to Esfahān. Subsequently, he embarked upon a building program that made Esfahān a capital city much praised by European travelers and gave rise to a proverbial expression in Iran to the effect that Esfahān is "half the world" owing to its beautiful bridges, avenues, palaces, mosques, and the like, many of which Shāh 'Abbās commissioned.

The most famous of his projects was the Shāh Square, at the south end of which the Shāh Mosque is situated.[11] The Shāh Square, which measures 500 meters in length and 140 meters in width, is one of the great squares of the world; it was designed as the venue for parades and reviews, polo matches, public executions, and receptions for foreign dignitaries. The first building constructed on the square by Shāh 'Abbās was a mosque built in 1602 and named "Shaykh Lotfollāh" in honor of his father-in-law. Its exterior dome, like that of the Shāh Mosque, is also used as inspiration for carpet field patterns, as is its interior dome, the design of which appears in carpets from Tabriz, Tehrān, and elsewhere. Shaykh Lotfollāh Mosque is on the east side of the square. On its west side is a porched pavilion

---

11. The Shāh Mosque is illustrated and discussed by Arthur Upham Pope, *Persian Architecture: The Triumph of Form and Color* (New York: Braziller, 1965), and by L. V. Golombek, "Anatomy of a Mosque," in *Iranian Civilization and Culture*, ed. Charles Adams, pp. 10–11. The Shāh Square is illustrated in Pope, *Persian Architecture*, pp. 206–216.

Figure 13. *Esfahān* arabesque medallion and field carpet.

five stories high that was built in 1609. Called Āli Qāpu, which means "lofty gate," it was designed for several purposes: as a royal reception hall, as a location from which to view the square, and as the gateway to the palace gardens and grounds behind it. Then, on the north end of the great enclosure, the inward-facing façade of which was completed in 1616, is the Qaysariyeh Bazaar.

But certainly the most impressive structure on the square is the Shāh Mosque on the south end; it looms as a magnificent backdrop to activities in the rest of the square. Begun in 1612, the Shāh Mosque was not completely ready for use until twenty years later. It took four years just to complete the portal that opened onto the square. Because the Shāh Mosque's decorations are the inspiration for contemporary Persian carpet patterns, some awareness of the significance of the Shāh Mosque as a building with a particular design, decoration, and function is important. If all aspects of the building are considered, the Shāh Mosque may, more than anything else, be a "reflection of the personality of its founder . . . , a monument to him," and an "embodiment of the concerns and ethos of monarchy."[12] But within a narrower perspective, the relationship between the Shāh Mosque and the carpets its decoration has inspired is obviously religious in nature.

In the decoration of the mosque sanctuary, a microcosm of the relationship between the universe and heaven is often represented. Often mosque domes, such as that of the Shāh Mosque, are decorated with sunburst or stellar designs by means of which the worshipper is brought into contact with heavenly bodies. The heavens are brought down to earth in such mosque architecture, unlike some Western church building styles that emphasize the building reaching through its spire(s) up to the heavens. In addition, the presence of trees and water in mosque courtyards and the use of floral elements in architectural decoration seem to indicate that "the mosque is a preview of paradise, a splendid garden," comparable in many ways to descriptions of heaven given in the Koran. The very entranceway to such a mosque is seen as a "gateway to salvation." An inscription on the Shāh Mosque entranceway reads: "I am the Prophet, City of Knowledge, 'Ali is the gate. He who wishes knowledge should come to the Gate." The sides of the entranceway extend outward to form wings that invite and embrace the

worshipper. The minarets reach into the sky toward heaven. The mosque sanctuary itself faces Mecca, the direction in which the faithful must face in prayer.[13]

These religiously inspired motifs and their symbolic significance are repeated in a variety of carpet patterns, among them several important types woven in Esfahān. As for the distinctiveness of the Esfahān medallion carpet design, the arabesques in the field are, as noted above, readily identifiable; what may not be so obvious, however, is that the arabesques in the field complement activity in the medallion, for the typical Esfahān medallion is constituted by arabesque vines and bifurcations that are paired, turned back on each other, and crisscrossed. Arabesque shapes have been used as varied themes in oriental carpets at least as early as the Turkish Ottoman era with its Lotto carpet types in which arabesques are stylized and paired in such a way as to create a latticework effect.[14] The field arabesques are clearly contrasted with the medallion shape; yet they are not intended to monopolize the observer's attention. Instead, they are part of a plan emanating from the medallion itself.

In addition, Esfahān medallion carpets exhibit another distinctive characteristic. Rather than being circumscribed by a line to reinforce their participation in a circular or polygonal medallion entity, the medallion tips reach out into the floral material of the field, almost merging with field elements and leading the observer's eyes outward from the medallion to the remainder of the field. In so doing, the medallion, no matter how bold it may be, does not monopolize attention either. Consequently, a sense of balance between field and medallion is reinforced by the fact that the outer tips or edges of the floral medallions, as in almost all curvilinear Persian carpets, occur in multiples of four. Perhaps this sense of balance results from the tension between the four lines of the rectangular field or the four right angles at the ends of those lines and the medallion tips, occurring in fours or multiples of four, which extend outward from the carpet's center.

Among other features of contemporary weaving in Esfahān are the fineness of weave, the closely clipped pile surface, the distinctive Esfahān red color, and the precise and feathery impression of the edges, tips, and lines of flowers and

12. Golombek, "Anatomy of a Mosque," pp. 9–10.

13. Ibid.
14. Kurt Erdmann, *Seven Hundred Years of Oriental Carpets*, pp. 56–60.

Figure 14. Heris medallion carpet.

leaves. Esfahān carpets are almost uniformly small in size, very finely woven, and quite traditional in their use of Safavid design inspiration. Silk or, more often today, fine mercerized cotton is used for the warp material, and sometimes silk rather than wool is used for the pile. The most popular designs are the arabesque medallion and field pattern; a similar medallion design lacking arabesques that is also woven in Nā'in in distinctive gray, silver, dark blue, and black colors; a one-directional, almost naturalistic garden scene carpet; and a garden scene prayer carpet (see Fig. 25).

Heris Medallion with Floral Field Carpet

Between the curvilinear and rectilinear extremes of Persian carpet design styles exemplified, respectively, by typical Kermān and Torkaman patterns are patterns that seem to exhibit influences of both. For example, formal "citified" versions of Bakhtiyāri compartment designs, often in silk, are made in Qom. (See Fig. 23.) Some Birjand carpets also seem to be a combination of the floral and the geometric in their characteristic *herāti* motif fields that are divided into field, medallion, and corner areas through the use of stepped lines and changes in the constituent colors of the motifs. Distinctive Josheqān and Hamadān medallion carpets (see Figs. 15, 17) are

other examples of carpet types exhibiting a mixture of characteristics, as is a popular and distinctive medallion pattern from the town of Heris (see Fig. 14).

Heris is located in the Turkish-speaking region of Āzarbāyjān about fifty miles east of Tabriz, but not on the main road.[15] As a name for carpets, it is also used to refer to the products of many small towns and villages around Heris proper. Perhaps the term "village carpet" might be used to describe the products of Heris itself and similar carpets woven in nearby Bakhshāyesh, Belvardi, Joravān, and Sarāb. Carpets from this area are hybrids of city and tribal features and therefore distinctive in several ways.

The most typical Heris design is a medallion with corner elements, a red field, and floral shapes which constitute the medallion and corner elements and fill the field. These features identify

15. The name *Heris*, which rhymes with "fleece," is usually spelled "Heriz" in English, even by Iranologists, e.g., Donald N. Wilber, "Heriz Silk Rugs: A Myth," *Oriental Rug Review* 2, no. 7 (October 1982): 4–5. One of the centers where Heris-style medallion carpets are woven is the town of Sarāb. In Persian, the adjective for "belonging to Sarāb" is "Sarābi"; this has turned into "Serapi" in English, the name by which the popular carpet type is best known.

the Heris carpet as a city carpet, as does the fact that most Heris weavers refer to some sort of cartoon in their weaving.[16] The floral shapes, medallions, and corner elements are, however, quite angular, almost rectilinear in some cases. This rectilinear effect is achieved through the use of bold, multiple transition lines around each motif. Such transition lines are reminiscent of those of Caucasus carpets, as is the manner in which the constituent elements of Heris medallions are shaped into one large medallion shape vis-à-vis the formation of the individual medallions in Caucasus multiple medallion field carpets. The Caucasus influence is the source of the tribal inspiration in the Heris carpet. It is an influence that is perfectly natural for traditional village and town weaving throughout Iranian Āzarbāyjān, which, after all, shares cultural traditions with Soviet Āzarbāyjān or the Caucasus, an area that Iran ceded to Czarist Russia in the treaties of Golestān (1813) and Torkmanchāy (1828). Traditional Caucasus designs are consciously adapted in several weaving centers in Iranian Āzarbāyjān, chief among them Ardabil and Meshkinshahr.

A further distinctive characteristic of many Heris carpets is their creation of an impression of depth or layering, a clear divergence from the norm in contemporary Persian carpet designs, which generally do not effect a foreground, middle ground, or background and generally do not give an impression of depth or layers within the field. The Esfahān medallion, for example, has tips that reach toward the field profusion of *shāh 'abbāsi* shapes but does not give the impression of being set down on top of the floral field. The same holds for many Qashqā'i *boteh* medallion design carpets. In contrast, such multiple levels in Safavid designs were a conscious part of carpet design: medallions were set over floral elements, vines, and tendrils, and other levels of floral systems, cloud bands, animals, and other shapes were also depicted.[17]

In the case of the Heris carpet, the use of both bold transition lines around medallions and the color white in critical places often creates the impression that the medallion is closest to the surface, with the angular flowers beneath it, and that the corner elements are another system beneath the flowers, which are, in turn, part of a larger polygon that divides the field into two areas.

16. Edwards, *The Persian Carpet*, pp. 64–65; Ford, *The Oriental Carpet*, pp. 266–267.

17. "Rugs and Carpets," *Encyclopaedia Britannica* 15th ed. (1974).

Figure 15. Maymeh Josheqān diamond cluster medallion carpet.

The Heris carpet is also one of those carpet types that succeed in integrating many bright colors. Consistent use of transition lines, usually of the same two or three colors throughout the carpet field, may account for the harmony achieved by an otherwise unharmonious combination of colors.

The Heris medallion design has been extremely popular in the United States, where the more formal and complicated curvilinear designs have not been generally as popular as simpler patterns. In the case of the Heris design, which is complicated, the fact of the angular effects achieved by bold and multiple transition lines may make the design seem less formal; the informality that observers sense is a natural part of many room environments in the United States where such Heris carpets have been used.

Josheqān Diamond Cluster Design Carpet

Josheqān is a town in the mountains to the east of the main Tehrān-Esfahān highway about seventy-five miles north of Esfahān. It is famous for a diamond cluster design, which is woven also in Maymeh and Kāshān. (See Fig. 15.) Maymeh, just off the Tehrān-Esfahān highway, is about twenty miles southwest of Josheqān. Kāshān is located not much farther from Josheqān than Maymeh, but in the opposite direction to the northeast on the other side of the mountains.

The Josheqān design is another hybrid design like Heris, Hamadān, Birjand, and Mazlaqān medallion carpets. It has obviously floral elements reminiscent of classical antique vase carpets with their clusters of flowers. The design also exhibits a field with a central medallion area and corner elements. Or the corner elements may be viewed as another level of field beyond the hexagonal shape that creates, with its stepped lines, the corner spandrels and merges with the inner border.

But the design principle behind the Josheqān carpet is the diamond shape. Each cluster of flowers is shaped like a diamond, as is the medallion. The large hexagonal field polygon may itself be a diamond with its left and right tips disappearing under the border. The design, thus, has curvilinear and rectilinear elements and is both city and tribal in inspiration. It does not quite become a compartment carpet, however, because the field color itself, rather than lines, creates the spaces between diamond floral clusters. These spaces likewise keep the design from seeming as busy as popular Rāvar designs where virtually no field color shows through the small bunches of flowers.

The Josheqān diamond-cluster design may seem at first glance uncomplicated or unsophisticated. Yet something in the design prevents the monotonous effect that perfect regularity might cause. The diamond clusters usually remain at constant angles with one another, but the diamond shape and the angles of the medallion and corner spandrels are different enough to create a rhythm or tension while the diamonds achieve their obvious harmony. A further characteristic of such carpets woven without recourse to a cartoon is a lack of uniformity among the constituent elements and motifs themselves, and their arrangement in patterns resulting in an impression of spontaneity. This lack of uniformity is not the same as a defect or ill-drawn figure. It is instead the natural result of hand-eye determination of figures and relationships. In village and tribal carpet designs, it helps to effect vitality.

In contrast, there is a new grade of finely woven Torkaman design carpet being produced in Herāt today from cartoons drawn by expert designers. Motifs are all exactly the same size and shape and placed at exactly the same intervals throughout the field. The net result of such uniformity is lifeless regularity in which the slight variations that weaving from memory would naturally involve and that would give character to spacing are lost.[18] Designs of such carpets, as well as those of some carpets from Romania, Pakistan, and India that adapt tribal patterns from elsewhere, are so regular as to reveal their total design message almost at first glance. Some Kāshān and Qom versions of the Josheqān design are likewise somewhat mechanical and too regular, although in Kāshān the design is apparently woven from memory.[19]

Figure 16. *Herāti* motif.

18. Reinhard Hübel, *The Book of Carpets*, p. 43, asserts: "Unsatisfactory and bloodless too are the 'nomad patterns' constructed from tracings or sketches, entirely devoid of any original, earthy power—quite apart from the inadequacy of the understanding and imitation of the designs."

19. V. F. Costello, *Kashan: A City and Region in Iran* (New York: Bowker, 1976), p. 125.

Hamadān Medallion with *Herāti* Field Carpet

The Hamadān region is one of the most important village and town weaving areas in Iran. The greater Hamadān area consists of more than six hundred villages of various sizes with a total population of nearly 600,000 people. The city of Hamadān itself has a population of nearly 180,000 people; it is located about five hours by car southwest of Tehrān on the main highway to the Kurdish city Kermānshāh (renamed Bākhtarān in 1982), some two hours farther west.

Almost six thousand feet above sea level at the foot of Mount Alvand, a peak of almost twelve thousand feet, today's Hamadān is situated on the site of Ecbatana, the capital city of the Medes who ruled most of the Iranian plateau in the sixth century BCE, making Hamadān Iran's oldest city. It was later a capital for both the Achaemenid (559–330 BCE) and Sāsānian (224–640 CE) empires. However, nothing of the city's pre-Islamic greatness remains. Its contemporary significance as a center for the production of traditional handicrafts cannot be traced back into history beyond the Middle Ages. Its most important surviving monument is the tomb of the scientist, physician, and philosopher Ebn-e Sinā, famous in the West as Avicenna.

The Hamadān weaving area and the *herāti* motif often featured in its carpets are both extremely important in the production of modern Persian carpets. (See Figs. 16, 17.) The *herāti* motif is a composite form of a central flower around which four stylized leaves are symmetrically arranged. It generally serves as the major or organizing motif in carpets with or without a medallion whose fields are repeat patterns of the *herāti* motif combined with a second repeated motif or cluster of motifs that serves as a transitional device from one *herāti* motif to the next.

It may be of significance that the *herāti* motif, the Torkaman Tekkeh *gol*, and the field pattern of most medallion carpets share a quincunx configuration. The most common medallion carpets, including popular Hamadān and Heris carpets, feature five major symmetrically placed elements in the rectangular field: a central medallion and four corner elements. The latter can be quarter medallions, full corner medallions, or corner pieces drawn with or without some inspiration from central medallion elements. The *herāti* and Torkaman Tekkeh *gol* motifs also feature a central part surrounded by four symmetrically placed elements. If such motifs were to appear singly in the field of a carpet, drawn large enough so that

Figure 17. Hamadān medallion with *herāti* field carpet.

the field borders would begin immediately beyond the four symmetrically placed outer pieces, the motifs would also create a quincunx field plan.

In typical Hamadān medallion carpets, the quincunx field plan is balanced by the quincunx plan of the *herāti* motifs which are repeated throughout the field.

Minā Khāni Design Carpets

The *minā khāni* motif, which was featured in nineteenth-century Bijār and other Kurdish carpets, consists of a symmetrical flower of one shape surrounded by four flowers of a second shape. Other flowers, tendrils, or vines provide the transition from one *minā khāni* motif to another in the creation of an overall repeat pattern. The term *minā khāni* is sometimes translated as "daisy." In contemporary carpet-weaving in Iran, the town of Varāmin, twenty-six miles southeast of Tehrān, is most associated with the *minā khāni* design. In pre-modern times, Varāmin was occupied by various tribal groups, including Lors and Kurds. The latter group provided the original inspiration for modern Varāmin *minā khāni* design carpets. (See Fig. 18.)

Although the motif originally had a tribal origin, it is currently used in town productions as indicated by the use of cotton warps and wefts, rather than wool. Its relationship to the *herāti* motif illustrated in the Hamadān medallion carpet is an indication both of its Kurdish origin and of its use in the quincunx sort of motif arrangement described above. However, in Varāmin carpets featuring the *minā khāni* motif, as in Torkaman carpets featuring an overall repeat pattern of five-part *gol*s as the major motif, there is no medallion plus corner elements to balance the quincunx nature of the field motif. In Kurdish

Figure 18. Varāmin *minā khāni* design carpet.

carpets, the *herāti* motif also often appears without any medallions.

Kurdish weaving from the traditional Kurdish region west of Hamadān and centering in such cities as Sanandaj and Kermānshāh (now Bākhtarān) is, of course, famous in its own right.[20] In addition, there is significant Kurdish weaving in places where the Kurds have been forced to resettle. Varāmin and the Quchān area in Khorāsān, two hours by car from Mashhad, are examples. The Kurds themselves are of particular significance to Iran insofar as they are an Indo-European people who settled in Iran several centuries before Islam. Most other tribal groups in Iran reached Iran in latter, Islamic times and are Turkic rather than Indo-European. By the Saljuq era in the eleventh century, the Kurdish homeland called Kordestān was referred to as a formal entity. Today, the Kurds number about five million; they are located in Turkey, Iraq, and northern Syria, as well as Iran. Many of them have nationalistic political aspirations, but their efforts at national unity or autonomy have been thwarted throughout this century by the central governments of the neighboring countries in which they live. In the case of the Iranian Kurds, whose handicrafts and traditional tribal culture and customs are quite important to Iran, many of them do not feel that they belong to the Persian Iranian culture that dominates the country, even though both groups are Indo-European in origin and language. The Kurds are for the most part Sunni Moslems,

whereas the official religion of Iran, even before the Islamic Republic, was Shi'ism.

Like some other Iranian tribal groups, the Kurds have long resisted attempts by the central government in Tehrān to control affairs in their territory and to centralize the country. In economic terms, many Kurdish settlements have had to succumb to pressures from Tehrān and even from abroad. For example, there is a common medallion carpet woven today in the important traditional Kurdish weaving center Bijār that features floral elements that are European in origin, as in the American style Kermān and Arāk patterns described earlier. In the case of the *herāti* motif, however, and the related *minā khāni*, patterns remain wholly traditional.

Afshār Multiple Medallion Carpet

Among various design types of rectilinear patterns that have tribal ancestry or affiliation, the multiple medallion design is very common in Iran. It appears in carpets of Afshār, Ardabil, Baluch, Karājeh, Meshkinshahr, and Yalameh provenance, among others. Basically, the design involves two or more geometric medallion shapes on the vertical axis in the carpet field with other design elements creating balance horizontally.

Afshār, Ardabil, Meshkinshahr, and Yalameh multiple medallion carpets may have a common source, since they all derive from Turkic weaving traditions associated primarily with the Caucasus. For example, the Afshār tribe was part of a tribal confederation in Āzarbāyjān centuries ago, although today the Afshārs and carpets referred to as Afshār are from the region to the immediate south and west of Kermān. The Afshārs came to the Kermān region as a result of forced migrations during the Safavid era (1501–1722) and also during the reign of Nāder Shāh, an Afshār who ruled over most of Iran from 1736 to 1747. He led the last major Iranian military campaign on foreign soil, a great depradatory invasion of India, from which he brought back the so-called Peacock Throne and other booty that subsequently have become famous as the Iranian Crown Jewels.

The Afshār carpets on the market today are produced by Afshār nomads and villagers, whose total number has been estimated at forty thousand, as well as by Persian villagers in places where Afshārs have settled. It might be more appropriate, therefore, to refer to the carpets in a general way as "Kermān area tribal design" carpets. But since their design origins are Afshār, the latter designation seems more natural, even

20. Erwin Gans-Ruedin, *The Splendor of Persian Carpets*, pp. 241–274, presents color plates and commentaries on sixteen mostly nineteenth-century Kurdish carpets. See also Robert Biggs, ed., *Discoveries from Kurdish Looms*, for illustrations and background information.

though many of the Afshār carpets may be woven by persons who have no traditional ties with the Afshārs. On the other hand, carpet experts specifically interested in exact carpet provenance may be able to determine specific locales of Afshār production in the region, chief among them the towns of Nayriz and Sirjān, between which most of the Afshār tribal peoples live, and such smaller places as Bāft, Bam, and Shahr-e Bābak. With warps and wefts of cotton, a sign of the influence of settled communities on tribal weaving, contemporary Afshār-design carpets continue a tradition with a known history of centuries.

In comparison with other Iranian tribal carpets, Afshār carpets are generally more nearly square in shape. Their palette of colors is distinctive: reds, blues, and white (as trim). The carpet field around the multiple medallions and the larger division of the field space into two areas within the smaller of which the medallions appear is generally filled with floral scatter, sometimes *boteh* shapes but often simple quatrefoils of one or two colors with another color filling in the spaces between the petals, creating an overall circular shape.

With a design that goes back a century or more, multiple diamond medallion Afshār carpets are a most common sort. (See Fig. 19.) As initially complicated as this Afshār design appears, a not unsophisticated principle of organization accounts for much of its appeal. In other words, as with most traditional Persian carpet designs, there is a major organizing principle which influences the observer's appreciation of the visual appeal of the design of the carpet.

At first glance, the most striking thing about such carpets is the arrangement of three white diamonds on the vertical axis. These diamonds are striking both because they lie in the center of the carpet and because their white color stands out in comparison with the typical Afshār blue and red of the stepped polygons surrounding them and further dividing the field space. In such an arrangement of diamond shapes, the observer can expect to discern the organizing principle of the overall pattern. There are several possibilities. First, diamond shapes might be used elsewhere in the carpet to balance and complement the central string of diamond medallions. Second, the medallion latchhooks might appear on other field shapes to create common design effects among different motifs. Third, the white color of the diamond medallions might be an organizing and unifying force through the whole carpet. While

Figure 19. Afshār multiple medallion carpet.

each of these characteristics contributes to the design of this Afshār piece, they are secondary to another feature of the diamond arrangement: the occurrence of *three* white diamonds. The field of this carpet is organized from the diamonds on the vertical axis to the outermost stepped polygon in terms of the balancing of elements in groups of threes. There are three pointed tips in horizontal rows at the top and bottom of the field in red. The blue stepped polygon juts out in threes at the top and bottom and along the left and right lengthwise sides. The whole pattern of this very typical and traditional modern Afshār carpet is integrated by the repetition of patterns of threes.

Caucasus-inspired Multiple Medallion Carpets

Of the design traditions which originated beyond Iran's borders and the sphere of Persian Iranian culture, the two which are most important in today's Persian carpets are the Torkaman and the Caucasus design traditions. The Torkaman tradition has its roots in the Central Asian weaving traditions of Oghuz tribes, while the Caucasus weaving traditions, famous today throughout the

Figure 20. Ardabil Caucasus-inspired medallion carpet.

world, flourished centuries ago in the Caucasus areas, towns, and cities of Dāghestān, Darband, Ganjeh, Kubā, and Shirvān. The weaving of the Caucasus peoples between the Black and Caspian seas has noticeably influenced weaving to the south on the Iranian side of the border, notably Afshār multiple medallion carpets; village and town weaving throughout the northwestern Iranian Āzarbāyjān provinces—Karājeh, for example; and much originally tribal weaving associated with Qashqā'i, Khamseh, and Yalameh peoples from the south-central Iranian province of Fārs.[21]

The most significant Caucasus-inspired carpet weaving in Iran takes place in the Āzarbāyjān sub-provincial capital city of Ardabil and the smaller city of Meshkinshahr located on the road from

21. Erwin Gans-Ruedin, *The Connoisseur's Guide to Oriental Carpets*, pp. 83–111. Ford, *The Oriental Carpet*, presents numerous plates and descriptions of Dāghestān, Erivan, Ganjeh, Kazak, Khonjoresk, Perepedil, and Shirvān carpets, especially in the chapter "Geometric Repeating Medallion Designs," pp. 208ff; Plates 468–474, 513–518.

Ardabil to Tabriz. Here and in surrounding villages modern versions of traditional Caucasus carpets are woven. The designs are mostly classical multiple medallion patterns. (See Fig. 20.) Ardabil and Meshkinshahr carpets feature a variety of grades and materials. There are at least three distinct densities of pile material: warps can be all cotton, cotton with an s or z ply of wool about it, or all wool. In comparison with traditional Caucasus designs, the Ardabil and Meshkinshahr products are characterized by a greater variety in sizes (although room-size carpets are not the norm) and experimentation in new color combinations made possible by the ready availability of good chrome dyes.

Ardabil and Meshkinshahr carpets became quite popular in the 1960s and 1970s. During this period they filled a gap in the domestic and export market which had been created because new Caucasus products were rarely marketed outside the USSR and older pieces were relatively expensive. Products of Iranian Āzarbāyjān, Ardabil and Meshkinshahr carpets are a continuation of the Caucasus tradition, although there is nothing tribal about their production. Like the Soviet Caucasus, Iranian Āzarbāyjān is a Turkish-speaking, Shi'i region. The two areas, politically divided

Figure 21. Yalameh compartment design carpet.

since the Golestān and Torkmanchāy treaties ceded them to Russia in the second and third decades of the nineteenth century, share a common culture of which Ardabil and Meshkinshahr carpets are one evidence.

Variety in color and designs in the use of geometric medallions, floral motifs, and animal figures are hallmarks of Ardabil carpets. The most typical pattern consists of a row of three geometric medallions on the vertical axis, complemented and balanced by smaller rectilinear figures moving horizontally across the carpet. The multiple rectilinear medallions are generally built up from simpler shapes around which a final line establishes the outer hexagonal or octagonal impression.

Besides patterns woven in Ardabil and Meshkinshahr, traditional weaving throughout rural Āzarbāyjān owes most of its design inspiration to the Caucasus. In such communities as Lambarān, Ahar, and Karājeh, Caucasus inspiration is evident, but it is neither as deliberate nor as exact as in Meshkinshahr and Ardabil carpets. For example, the Karājeh carpet in its most typical design features a distinctive red field color, not typical of Ardabil and Meshkinshahr carpets. The town of Karājeh lies just off the road from Ardabil to Tabriz. Due east of Karājeh is Heris, a more famous town and weaving area known for its distinctive medallion carpets. In the most familiar Karājeh design, three geometric medallions on the vertical axis are surrounded by smaller flowers and floral scatter that, more than creating horizontal balance, fill up space. Further, the medallions are usually bounded by latchhooks or other outward moving lines that create a sunburst effect not typical of Ardabil and Meshkinshahr carpets. A second Karājeh design uses the typical multiple medallions reduced in size and repeated throughout the field to constitute an overall repeat pattern.

Interestingly, in a region far from Āzarbāyjān, Yalameh carpets exhibit similar multiple medallion and repeat medallion patterns. The Yalameh people are Lors or Qashqā'i-related and live in villages around Shāhrezā in south-central Iran. One of their distinctive designs is a garden compartment carpet, a type similar in overall design to the neighboring Bakhtiyāri garden compartment carpets, but the treatment of the compartment material in the Yalameh version is very different. Yalameh carpets are bright and rich in color with greens, oranges, and crimson. Red is not a typical field color. (See Fig. 21.)

The most distinctive Yalameh pattern, usually found in smaller carpets, features multiple medallions on the vertical axis, generally bounded with latchhooks. The field space around the medallions is generally filled with simpler stellate and rosette floral shapes not unlike the minor field motifs in some Qashqā'i carpets. The whole design is, however, obviously influenced by Caucasus weaving tradition.

Bakhtiyāri Garden Compartment Design Carpet

The Bakhtiyāris are the most famous of the Lor tribes whose traditional lands extended from Shirāz north to Esfahān and west to boundaries near Kermānshāh and Dezful. The Bakhtiyāris' traditional language is a dialect of an Iranian language called Lori. But Bakhtiyāri pile carpet weaving today does not reflect the traditions of tribal life. Bakhtiyāri weaving, which takes place near the city of Esfahān, even includes a version in typical Bakhtiyāri blues, reds, and whites of the Esfahān arabesque floral medallion with floral and arabesque field carpet design. Very simply, according to the experts: "The disruptions in tribal life caused by the gradual integration of the nomads into the mainstream of the social and economic life of Iran and their consequential tendency to settle or to emigrate to the cities, have

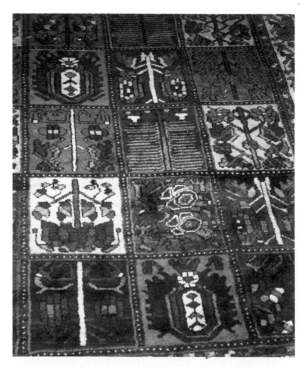

Figure 22. Bakhtiyāri garden compartment carpet.

produced an accelerated obsolescence of tribal customs."[22]

Thus it is that the Bakhtiyāri garden compartment carpet, perhaps the most traditional design woven by one of the most traditional Iranian tribal groups, now appears with cotton warps and wefts, where wool would be expected, a sure sign of town and city influence on tribal weaving.

Despite the fact that Bakhtiyāri carpets are woven today for commercial reasons, they are still heir to perhaps the oldest known oriental carpet pattern, and the fact of their popularity, including the inspiration behind more citified versions woven in Qom (see Fig. 23) and natural undyed wool versions woven in Tabriz, makes them a culturally significant traditional carpet.

The Bakhtiyāri compartment design features rectangles, squares, diamonds, lozenges, ogives, and other enclosed forms in which mostly floral material is presented. There are willow and cypress tree motifs, single *boteh* shapes in individual panels, clusters of *shah 'abbāsi* motifs, flowers, and the like. The arrangement of such garden elements in compartments dates back to the Pazyryk carpet, woven some 2,500 years ago, the oldest known oriental carpet in existence. The Pazyryk carpet (discussed in Chapter 2) features a field of twenty-four relatively square field compartments in six vertical and four horizontal rows. Each of the compartments features the same quatrefoil motif, and the whole field would seem to represent a formal garden.

The use of the formal garden as the basis of Persian carpet design was also an important part of urban, court-sponsored weaving in the fifteenth and sixteenth centuries. Many garden carpets of that era exhibit a cruciform of water courses or irrigation streams, often with fish swimming in them. On the banks of these streams are garden plots with various trees and floral motifs often represented rectilinearly. The Safavid garden compartment carpet is almost an aerial view of a formal Persian garden.[23]

Today's Bakhtiyāri garden compartment carpet (see Fig. 22) is heir to both Pazyryk and Safavid compartment carpets as well as to one of the most obvious and distinctive patterns of what almost

Figure 23. Qom Bakhtiyāri design carpet.

all Persian carpets represent, however stylized or geometric at first glance: a perfect garden.

In terms of classification, the Bakhtiyāri carpet has one other significant feature. It is usually one-directional. It can be axially symmetrical on the vertical axis, which means its left lengthwise half may be identical to its right lengthwise half, but the presence of cypress and willow trees, among other motifs, makes the top half unlike the bottom. This means that, viewed from the top end, some of the field material appears upside down, as is also true for two other important Persian carpet types, the figure or portrait carpet and the prayer carpet.

Modern Persian Figure or Portrait Carpets

There are furniture problems with almost all one-directional Persian carpet designs intended as floor coverings in room settings because much of the design will appear upside down to the

22. Amedeo de Franchis and John T. Wertime, *Lori and Bakhtiyāri Flatweaves: An Exhibition Held at the Iran-American Society* (Tehrān: Tehran Rug Society, March 1976), p. 12.

23. Kurt Erdmann, *Seven Hundred Years of Oriental Carpets*, pp. 66–70. Other color plates of such formal

garden carpets appear in Ian Bennett, ed., *Complete Illustrated Rugs and Carpets of the World*, p. 75; Ford, *The Oriental Carpet*, pp. 144–155; Gans-Ruedin, *The Splendor of Persian Carpets*, p. 32; and Daniel Walker, *Oriental Rugs of the Hajji Babas* (New York: Asia Society and Harry N. Abrams, 1982), p. 74, Plate 20.

observer from the opposite direction. The most problematic of the one-directional designs is the portrait or figure carpet, which seems better suited as a wall hanging than as a floor covering. In the 1960s and 1970s, portraits of Mohammad Rezā Pahlavi, Farah Dibā Pahlavi, and John F. Kennedy appeared in smaller carpets. Among larger carpets featuring more than one person, the design is often an idyllic or romantic scene. Such portrait or figure carpets are woven mostly in Tabriz and Esfahān and need to be very finely woven in order for the figures to be distinctly rendered. (See Fig. 24.)

One popular scene depicted in such carpets is a tableau which one might associate with these famous stanzas from Edward FitzGerald's *The Rubáiyát of Omar Khayyám*:

With me along the strip of Herbage strown
That just divides the desert from the sown,
Where name of Slave and Sultan is forgot—
And Peace to Mahmud on his golden Throne!

A Book of Verses underneath the Bough,
A Jug of Wine, a loaf of Bread—and Thou
Beside me singing in the Wilderness—
Oh, Wilderness were Paradise enow!

Based on Persian quatrains attributed to the historical figure of 'Omar Khayyām (d. 1123), FitzGerald's famous English poem is very Persian in content.[24] Its speaker, an imaginary Khayyām, voices a perennial Iranian view. Although figure carpets that present Khayyāmic scenes are not traditional textile patterns but rather attempts to create the effects of a painting through weaving, their popularity in Iran apparently has to do with the Persianness of their content: the perfectly idyllic riverside scene of friends or lovers. As described in the next chapter, even the most typical Iranian patterns, such as the Kermān, Torkaman, Heris medallion, and Bakhtiyāri garden compartment carpets have the same import, in the context of which the fact that the English word "paradise" has the same origin as the Persian word *ferdows*, which refers to a perfect garden in this world or in the next, is not insignificant.

Persian portrait or figure carpets also serve as a springboard for an observation about the representation of human and animal figures in Islamic art, discussed in some detail in the next chapter. From the sixteenth century onward, numerous carpet types produced in royal manufactories exhibited animal and human figures as well as angels and mythological creatures. In light of the popular notion that Islam, as a firm monotheistic reaction to pre-Islamic polytheism and idolatry in Arabia, forbade the representation of human figures in its pictorial art, these portrait, figure, hunting, and animal carpet designs are indirect evidence that from the Safavid era to the end of the Pahlavi dynasty, that is from 1501 through 1978, religion was somehow subservient to political institutions.[25] Thus, royal courts upon whose patronage arts and crafts depended and which commissioned the production of carpets and the like were able by virtue of their power over the religious establishment to ignore strictly religious attitudes and opposition whenever they wished, especially since their art was intended for their own circles and not for the public at large.

A final note on such figure carpets is that they, along with some garden scene designs also woven in Tabriz, Esfahān, Nā'in, and Qom, are not even axially symmetrical. Most traditional carpet designs are biaxially symmetrical: the left half mirrors the right half, and the top half mirrors the bottom. One-directional carpets, such as many prayer and garden compartment carpet designs, are generally axially symmetrical: the left half of the design mirrors the right half. But the portrait and figure carpets, as well as some garden scene carpets, are not symmetrical in any direction. This atypicality in textile design principles, as well as the obvious transfer of subject material from printing to the carpet surface, has convinced some experts that modern portrait or figure carpets have no authenticity or beauty.[26]

24. John W. Draper, "FitzGerald's Persian Local Color," *West Virginia University Bulletin: Philological Papers* 14 (1963): 26–56.

25. As Erdmann, "Figure Carpets," in *Seven Hundred Years of Oriental Carpets*, p. 71, argues, in early Islam there was no doctrine forbidding the representation of living forms in art; and portrayal of human figures was always a significant feature of the Islamic art of Iran. For more on this issue, see K. A. C. Creswell, "The Lawfulness of Painting in Early Islam," *Islamic Culture* 24 (1950): 218–225; and Oleg Grabar, "Architecture and Art," in *The Genius of Arab Civilization*, ed. John R. Hayes (New York: New York University Press, 1975), pp. 93–95.

26. Donald N. Wilber, "The Triumph of Bad Taste: Persian Pictorial Rugs," *Hali* 2 (1979): 192–197; Ford, "Picture Designs; Animal and Bird Designs," in *The Oriental Carpet*, pp. 156–168. Rita Reif, "Maggie and Jigs Flying High Aboard a Persian Rug," *The New York Times* (March 24, 1978), describes and illustrates an Iranian figure carpet owned by the cartoonist George McManus depicting his comic strip characters.

Figure 24. Esfahān figure carpet.

Prayer Carpets

Prayer carpet designs are among the most traditional one-directional Persian carpet patterns. Uniformly depicting an indentation or arch shape in the upper field area, these carpet designs can be traced back to at least the fifteenth century. One is depicted, for example, in a Timurid miniature painting dated 1436.[27]

The distinctive arch shape in many prayer carpet fields is assumed to represent the *mehrāb* or arch shape built into that wall of a mosque that faces Mecca, Islam's holiest city and the site of the famous *hajj* pilgrimage that attracts millions of Moslems every lunar year. In addition, Moslems must face Mecca in performing their compulsory daily ritual prayers. Iranian Shi'i Moslems perform these prayers, which involve standing, bowing, and prostrating oneself while reciting memorized prayers in Arabic, at dawn, noon, and dusk. Prayer carpets both incorporate a reminder of the duty to pray in the *mehrāb* shape and provide the Moslem with a clean surface on which to pray after performing compulsory ritual ablutions.

The Persian terms for "prayer carpet" are *sajjādeh* and *jānamāzi*. The word *sajjādeh* comes from Arabic and means the cloth or carpet upon which the prescribed prostration called *sajdeh* is performed. The term *jānamāzi* means simply something, that is, a cloth or rug, which constitutes the place (*jā*) where the ritual prayer (*namāz*) is performed. Persian prayer carpets are woven in tribal, village, and urban settings all over the country of Iran. Torkaman, Baluch (see Fig. 36), and Zābol prayer carpets are found in the east and southeast. In the central part of the country, prayer carpets are woven in Esfahān and Kāshān. Distinctive prayer carpets are woven in the northwestern city of Tabriz. Qom prayer carpets are one of the many distinctively rendered patterns woven in that city.

Situated ninety miles south of Tehrān on the main road to Esfahān, Qom is the religious center of Iran. In existence from perhaps pre-Islamic times, Qom became a pilgrimage site when Emām Rezā's sister Ma'sumeh Fātemeh died there in 816. In the early years of the seventeenth century, Shāh 'Abbās the Great built a great shrine in Qom in her honor. Today Qom is the center of Shi'i Moslem theological studies in Iran.

27. Wilhelm von Bode, revised by Ernst Kühnel, *Antique Rugs from the Near East*, 4th rev. ed., trans. C. G. Ellis, Figure 115.

Figure 25. Esfahān garden scene prayer carpet.

As a religious center with a population of over 250,000 people, Qom could be expected to produce obviously religious carpets. Ironically, however, many Qom carpet types are among the most secular of Persian carpet styles and patterns. The influence of religion on the Qom weaving industry is more a matter of the fact that the cottage craft is there carried out by women with looms in their homes in a city in which they are expected not to be part of public business enterprises.

Interestingly, there seem to be no traditional designs and patterns associated with Qom. In fact, pile carpet weaving did not develop on a large scale in Qom until the 1930s, when a number of Kāshān merchants set up the industry there. However, carpets woven in Qom, no matter which pattern or size, are distinctive in style, appearance, and feel. They are almost always finely woven with fine mercerized cotton or silk warps and either wool or silk pile. When silk is used, it may be only to highlight certain floral shapes in an otherwise wool pile or it may be used for all of the pile.

Figure 26. Qom gateway prayer carpet.

Qom carpets feature designs adopted and adapted from elsewhere. Among them are Bakhtiyāri compartment patterns (see Fig. 23), the Josheqān diamond medallion and diamond floral cluster design carpet, Esfahān medallion with floral field patterns, Kermān floral medallion with plain field designs, garden scenes à la Tabriz and Esfahān, and the *afshān* design associated with Kāshān weaving. In almost all cases, the Qom carpet is formal, citified, luxurious, and expressive of affluence. Often, variations of traditional designs originating elsewhere are drawn with modern elements, such as stylized flowers and vases. The most expensive Persian carpets on the average per foot, Qom carpets seem most appropriate in the very sort of secular, formal, lavish entertaining settings to which the city of Qom itself, as the theological center of Iran, seems so clearly opposed.

Even Qom gateway prayer carpet designs seem less an invitation to religious piety than a luxuriant secular floral display in a gateway setting over which the suggestion of a *mehrāb* shape is depicted. (See Fig. 26.)

4. Symbolism in Modern Persian Carpet Designs

Many oriental carpet experts view Persian carpet designs as merely or purely decorative in their combination of shapes, motifs, and colors.[1] But according to one expert:

It would really be well to throw the phrase "mere decoration" right out of the window, and to wake up to the fact that the most significant proportions and rhythms, whether universal, physical or tragical-comical-historical, [or] pastoral, have been expressed in all serious and masterly decoration. The sheer mental power which goes into great decoration is not expended for the "titillation of the senses" any more than great music is elaborated for that purpose. . . . The difficult creation of varied form so as to make us feel both more profoundly and more highly than we usually do really operates at the contemplative level, and involves us in a calculus to which we are very little accustomed. But shape and color, quantity (size of figure and field, intensity of hue), quality (the energy, calm, antiquity, joyousness, solemnity, of a particular shape or hue in its surroundings), dynamics (the systems of felt forces which govern these rugs: the answer of a corner-spandrel to a medallion; the insight underlying apparent caprice in the "displacement" of decorative figure within the field, etc.), all the categories within which the painter's self-dedication is carried out, today as before, are illustrated by these masterpieces.[2]

"Masterpieces" here means classical antique carpets. For even those experts who are open to the possibility of symbolism in Persian carpets generally argue that if oriental carpets were ever meaningful or symbolically represented concepts and attitudes, it was in the distant past, when traditional values and a traditional world view were still understood consciously by people who represented them and appreciated their representation in art.[3]

One obvious feature of this volume in its focus on contemporary Persian carpets is its advocacy of appreciation of modern Persian carpets as opposed to the general sentiment among Persian carpet experts that the superiority of Safavid and Qājār classical antiques renders contemporary carpets almost unworthy of serious appreciation by comparison. In its attempt to demonstrate that the traditional designs of many modern Persian carpets embody symbolism, this chapter is part of the argument for appreciating the aesthetic appeal of those carpets. The reader is advised that such a view is not a popular one. In any case, whatever one's beliefs, a starting point in considering the possibilities might be conventional features of carpet designs.

Conventionalism in Persian Carpet Designs

Among the numerous conventional aspects of Persian carpet-weaving, two are particularly significant to the issues of symbolism in modern Persian carpet designs. First is the fact that most Persian carpets achieve their design effects through the use of six to twelve colors, often bright. A motif of one or more colors is bounded by a line of another color that serves as a transition between it and the next motif or the background color. In short, when one thinks of a Persian carpet, images of vivid colors first come to mind. Second, almost all Persian carpets depict plant or floral

1. E.g., according to Arthur Cecil Edwards, *The Persian Carpet*, p. 51: "The end which they [the Persians] had in view was delight through symmetry and beauty but no more. During the years I spent in Persia I never heard any reference to symbolism in carpet design." According to Sirus Parhām, *Qāli-ye Bolvardi*, p. 29: "The beauty of an oriental carpet is more a matter of feeling and enjoying than understanding. If we look otherwise at this noble Eastern art . . . we'll be led astray" (my translation). Parhām also relates an interview with an eighty-two-year-old Bolvardi weaver who told him that she had never heard anyone in the process of teaching someone else how to weave say anything about the meaning of designs.

2. Eric Schroeder, "The Art of Looking at Rugs," in *McMullan Exhibition*, pp. 11–12.

3. E.g., Schuyler Cammann, "Symbolic Meanings in Oriental Rug Patterns: I, II, III," *Textile Museum Journal* 3, no. 3 (December 1972): 5–54.

forms, however stylized. The floral forms are depicted as perfectly beautiful and arranged in or-
dered, symmetrical patterns. These two conventional aspects of Persian carpet design suggest
an aesthetic common to carpets and other traditional forms of Iranian art while highlighting
something of what Iranian art has traditionally
had to say about Iran. For example, traditional
Iranian art of different periods is generally held
to exhibit three basic features. First, there is a
"strong stress on color, which presents itself in
nearly every form of art." Second, there is "a tendency for highly stylized form and even for ab-
straction which manifests itself in the countless
arabesque decorations in carpets, tile decorations,
and manuscript illumination." Third, Iranian art is
traditionally idealistic, which is to say it trans-
figures "life to a higher plane" so that the observer is "thus never aware of poverty, personal
or political stresses, or even the terrible condi-
tions that the countless wars and changes of dynasties must have brought about in the country
and to its inhabitants." What is generally presented "is an enchanted world shown in the most
harmonious possible fashion and playing in a
realm that is well removed from everyday life."[4]

Exhibiting these traditional characteristics of
Iranian art, Persian carpets are a paean to color, a
vivid display of sometimes naturalistic but mostly
stylized plant and floral forms, an appeal to an
impersonal vision of order, precision, and rationality, and the epitome of rich decoration.

The significance of vivid colors and floral
forms in Persian carpets can obviously be viewed
as the expression or vision of an ideal environment by people whose physical surroundings
have relatively little colorful floral beauty in
them. As one writer observes in a discussion of
Qashqā'i carpets: "These fabric gardens, besides
fulfilling a useful function, rest the eye in a hot,
dry, dazzling, and at times inhospitable land."[5]
The Persian carpet, whether of tribal, village, or
urban provenance, captures this vision of green-
ery and floral beauty or of the fleeting reality of
spring, the one season when the environment
approaches the ideal, and preserves it in the tent
or house.

The display of rationality, order, and calm in
Persian carpet patterns may suggest the importance of these qualities for peoples whose society
has historically experienced continuing uncertainty and periodic chaos as a result of a series of
devastating invasions, from Alexander's 2,300 years
ago to Iraq's in 1980, and of such catastrophic natural disasters as frequent earthquakes, winter avalanches, and springtime floods. In addition, there
has been the traditional social and political order
deriving from the absolute authority of local land-
lords and tribal khāns to royal fiat. A vision of
order and calm in the designs of the most common and conspicuous piece of furniture in Iranian homes of all sorts would seem a much de-
sired or needed contrast with the very different
sort of world beyond the walls of those homes.

The impersonality of the vision of perfect
natural beauty in a context of perfect order and
rationality exhibited by many carpet designs sug-
gests aspects of a traditional religious and social
order characterized by a lack of significance attached to individual effort and the individual
voice addressing itself to individual rights, needs,
emotions, and views. In Persian literature, the
most revered traditional Iranian art form, this
same impersonality is manifest. As one Iranian
scholar observes:

For centuries and centuries Persian literature remained, so to say, impersonal. The artist was always
supposed to follow the lines which had been laid
down before him, and to produce a work in the admit-
ted and respected social cadre. He could seldom be
seen in his work; he was to follow the precepts of
accepted morality, and exigencies of his readers who
were exclusively members of the ruling class and of
the intellectual elite.[6]

As for carpet designs as the epitome of rich
decoration, their conventional design effects
seem to parallel distinctively Persian Iranian ritual and formal aspects of social intercourse by
which a person can demonstrate ritual hospitality
and thoughtfulness, obscure individual emotions
and thoughts seen not to be efficacious, and
maintain individual privacy. This system, desig-
nated by the Persian term ta'ārof, is a pervasive,
core element of urban Persian Iranian culture;
it is discussed in Chapter 5 in conjunction with
a description of a typical Kāshān afshān design
carpet.

4. Richard Ettinghausen, "An Introduction to
Modern Persian Painting," in *Iran Faces the Seventies*,
(New York: Praeger, 1971), p. 344.

5. Pierre Oberling, *The Qashqā'i Nomads of Fārs* (The
Hague and Paris: Mouton, 1974), p. 68. This volume
includes maps of Fārs province, southern approaches
to Shirāz, and Qashqā'i summer and winter quarters.

6. Sa'id Nafisi, "A General Survey of the Existing
Situation in Persian Literature," *Bulletin of the Institute
of Islamic Studies*, no. 1 (1957): 15–16.

If the possibilities relating to the colorfulness, floral content, rationality, impersonality, and decorativeness of traditional Iranian carpet patterns have had something to do with Persian carpets and their appeal in the past, and if many Iranians today feel particularly at home or comfortable with such traditional carpet patterns, the import of such carpets would seem to remain relevant. Such possibilities are evidence against the commonplace assumption that Persian carpet designs in modern Persian carpets are purely decorative.

In fact, it is unlikely for several reasons that the traditional craft of carpet-weaving on the Iranian plateau, unlike traditional arts and crafts elsewhere in the world, has embodied no symbolic content in design elements and their patterning or that it does not give voice to a culture-specific world view.

First, even visual art that seems primarily decorative may, as suggested above, have significance and meaning as such. In the case of Persian carpets, such significance is communicated through the proportions and rhythms created by means of such elements as color, the dynamics of motifs, and spacing.[7]

Second, a response to the commonplace view that many Persian carpet designs are merely decorative because they are apparently abstract is the potential significance or meaning behind geometric forms and patterns. For much of Islamic art, of which Persian carpets constitute an important later medium, may be interpreted as "a means of relating multiplicity to unity by means of mathematical forms which are seen, not as mental abstractions, but as reflections of the celestial archetypes within both the cosmos and the minds and souls of men."[8] Specifically, in the view of some Islamic art historians, Moslem artists traditionally "explored all the geometric systems that depend upon the regular division of the circle," a method asserted to be "no more than a symbolic way of expressing *towhid* [divine unity]."[9]

Third, there are numerous examples of individual Persian carpets or carpet types in which specific motifs or patterns can be presumed to have meaning. For example, there is an early-twentieth-

century carpet from Meshkinshahr[10] in which a stylized tree creating diamond or hexagonal polygons on the vertical axis is depicted, together with simple figures, including barnyard animals, children, and a man on a horse. Supposing the weaver to be a woman, one can view this carpet as her snapshot of the happy reality of a moment in village life or as her painting of wished-for prosperity and abundance, a sort of daydream in which the tree, itself a symbol of life and greenness, organizes the scene.

Another example of the meaning of motifs is the use of lion figures as field motifs in various Persian carpet types.[11] One of them is a traditional

---

7. Schroeder, "The Art of Looking at Rugs," pp. 9–13.

8. Sayyed Hosayn Nasr, in Keith Critchlow, *Islamic Patterns: An Analytical and Cosmological Approach* (New York: Schocken Books, 1976), p. 6.

9. Titus Burckhardt, in Issam El-Said and Ayşe Parman, *Geometric Concepts in Islamic Art* (London: World of Islam Festival, 1976), pp. ix–x.

10. Reinhard Hübel, *The Book of Carpets*, p. 171, Plate 14.

11. P. R. J. Ford, *The Oriental Carpet*, pp. 164–165, Plate 3, depicts a lion (and other animals) in a Qashqā'i *gabeh* rug. Jenny Housego, *Tribal Rugs*, p. 98, Plate 78, presents a Qashqā'i lion rug. Hübel, *The Book of Carpets*, p. 217, Plate 103, presents an early-twentieth-century Lor carpet: "The life-size tiger, bleeding at the neck, and destroying the pattern by its disproportionate size, is intended to avert unknown, fearsome dangers from the tent." R. E. G. Macey, *Oriental Prayer Rugs*, Plate 54, presents a prayer rug depicting four lions prominent in the lower half of the field. Joseph V. McMullan in collaboration with Donald O. Reichart, *The George Walter Vincent and Belle Townsley Smith Collection of Islamic Rugs* (Springfield, Mass.: George Walter Vincent Smith Art Museum, n.d.), Plate 3, presents a Kermān rug which features "a grotesque rendition of a famed and frequently used motif in Persian art, the fight between the lion and the bull. The devices can be termed Day (the lion's sun-like face) and Night (the bull's horns resembling the curve of the new moon). These devices are frequently used in various ways but always show the king represented by the lion, or often the griffin, as the victor."

The exhibition catalogue *Lion Rugs from Fārs* features forty-one plates together with descriptions of Qashqā'i, Khamseh, Bakhtiyārī, and Lor carpets featuring one or more lion figures as major motifs in the field pattern. In a foreword, Richard Ettinghausen describes the Iranian lion as follows: "As the noblest and most powerful of the animals, he was regarded as the traditional adversary of kings and as such he was shown in battle on the reliefs of Persepolis, on Sāsānian silver plates, and in sixteenth century Persian Hunting Carpets. . . . As the feline was always associated with kings, it naturally became a royal symbol when shown by itself or it connoted at least great courage and power. Hence Persian or Arabic words for 'lion' appear in combination in male names, and the image of the animal was applied as a suitable symbol on the carpets which the tribal women knotted for the tents of their chieftain or with him in mind even if they were to be used for their own, personal, purposes."

sort of Qashqā'i and Khamseh tribal carpet in which the lion figure or figures are presumably depicted as a tribute to guests who may be in a tent in which such a carpet is spread on the floor. However, in one distinctive and unusual lion scene, a lonely, singularly unregal lion is standing in an expanse of red, far from a star depicted in the middle of the field.[12] The carpet, in this case, seems to communicate a sense of the insignificance of the individual or of the meaninglessness of life. Such a theme is unusual not only for lion rugs, but for Persian rugs in general, in which an ideal world, not the real world with its problems and hardships, is almost always depicted. In this lion rug, a weaver has given a most personal and individual impress to a traditional subject.

The Lion, the Hunt, and Royal Themes

In Iranian mythology the lion is the "king of beasts" much as it is in Western cultures. At the Achaemenid ruins at Persepolis, on brick panels from Susa, in Sāsānian art, and on gates, funerary sculpture, and elsewhere in art from almost all periods of Iranian history, there are regal lion figures. The first nineteenth-century postage stamps issued by the Iranian government featured lion figures framed within floral borders certainly inspired by carpet border and manuscript illumination designs. The Iranian Constitution of 1906 declared that the official Iranian flag should consist of a field of three stripes—green, red, and white—on which were centered a golden lion and the sun emerging over the lion's back. This insignia was similar to those described as an Iranian army banner in the story "Sohrāb" in Ferdowsi's *Shāhnāmeh*, the monumental eleventh-century narrative that is the Persian Iranian national epic. Later miniature paintings depict similar banners decorated with lion-and-sun insignia. The same device appears on Safavid and Qājār coins, with lion figures by themselves on earlier coins. The lion and sun also appear as a sign of the zodiac on Iranian art objects from various historical periods. The Pahlavi era (1925–1979) national relief organization along the lines of the Red Cross was called "The Red Lion and Sun."[13] In these and other ways, then, the lion figure has been a familiar image in Persian art

and culture and has served as a symbol of the Persian Iranian nation or the Persian Iranian king.

But the lion has not always represented Iran or royalty. For example, some ancient Achaemenid seals depict the king fighting with and defeating a lion;[14] here the lion clearly does not symbolize the king. At the same time, not any animal would be the perfect enemy for the Iranian king. Only "the king of beasts" is a worthy royal combatant. Furthermore, the king probably should not appear to be fighting the lion with any overly large or powerful weapon. Because the king is all powerful and even God-like, he can fight the lion, for example, with his bare hands. These pictures on Achaemenid seals from 2,500 years ago presumably reminded their original viewers how powerful the king was and why he warranted obedience.

Such scenes in Achaemenid art may have been somewhat realistic, since there were lions on the Iranian plateau at that time. But the scene is not based on natural fact when it occurs in contemporary Iranian art, since there have been no sightings of lions in Iran for half a century. Why scenes of the king fighting lions are still important in Persian carpets today has to do in part with the continuing relevance of kingship or of attitudes pertinent to ruler-subject relations, regardless of the fact that kings no longer rule Iran.

It happens that the hunting carpet is a common and significant example of a particular subject matter that had meaning for Iranians in their traditional culture and appears still to be a natural, comfortable part of their visual living environment. It is a most traditional sort of carpet popular in modern Tabriz versions whose patterns derive from sixteenth-century Safavid hunting carpets. Four sixteenth-century Persian hunting carpets are particularly famous and are considered masterpieces of carpet-weaving. They are the Milan hunting carpet, the Hapsburg hunting carpet in Vienna, the hunting carpet in the Royal Palace Collection in Stockholm, and the hunting carpet in the Boston Museum.[15]

What is important about these Safavid carpets and thus about modern carpets they have inspired is the demonstrable association between

---

12. *Lion Rugs from Fārs*, p. 39, Plate 11.

13. Roger Savory, "Land of the Lion and Sun," *Islam and the Arab World*, ed. Bernard Lewis (New York: Alfred A. Knopf and American Heritage, 1976), pp. 245–272.

14. Photographs of several such seals appear in Jim Hicks et al., *The Persians* (New York: Time-Life Books, 1975), pp. 79–80.

15. For discussion of these famous carpets see Kurt Erdmann, "Figure Carpets," in *Seven Hundred Years of Oriental Carpets*, pp. 71–75; and Maurice S. Dimand, "Persian Hunting Carpets of the Sixteenth Century," *Boston Museum Journal* 69, nos. 355–356 (1971): 15–20.

Figure 27. Fārs lion rug.

and themes in their hunting scenes. For example, on the Boston hunting carpet there are "four states of huntsmanship":

> At the lowest range is a young man, apparently a prince and a novice at the game, who just manages to kill a rabbit. For this he uses a mace, so that one might say that this little scene stands for the Safavid form of "over-kill." The next stage is represented by a man who is older and more experienced than the rabbit-killer; he is seen piercing a fleet gazelle with a spear. He in turn is bested by a third, who slays another fast game animal at close range with his sword. But the supreme act of courage and physical force is achieved by a hunter who is shown combatting a lion bare-handed and slaying it.[17]

This bare-handed lion-hunter is the monarch, the epitome of courage and strength.

The facts that the Boston hunting carpet was produced and used by the court and that its medallion indicated the place of honor at which the royal personage sat imply that the carpet was both a tribute to him and a message to his visitors: the king represents ideals and perfection, and others, having less power than he, should know their place.

The naturalness and frequency of representation of hunting scenes in modern Persian carpets for Iranians personally unfamiliar with hunting or with lions would seem to imply the persisting expectedness of traditional ruler-subject relationships in Iran. Such a contention does not mean, however, that the specific message about kingship in the Safavid prototypes of such carpets is appreciated or that in those thousands of Iranian homes in which hunting carpets can be found, the Iranians who observe and enjoy the hunting scenes ever think about these carpets in these terms.

The scenes depicted in modern Tabriz hunting carpets (see Fig. 28) are much simplified in comparison with those in Safavid hunting carpets. Some of them lack medallion and corner elements and are simply one-directional repeat de-

them and royalty. First, the very theme of the hunting carpets is royal. Throughout recorded history on the Iranian plateau, hunting has been a royal occupation or diversion and practice for maintenance of martial skills. A particularly famous Sāsānian monarch was Bahrām, who ruled from 421 to 439 CE. He was called Bahrām "Gur" (*gur* meaning "wild ass" or "onager") because of his legendary skill at hunting onagers.[16] Furthermore, these hunting carpets depict various stages

---

16. Bahrām's legendary fame is part of the point to a famous Persian quatrain attributed to 'Omar Khayyām. Sādeq Hedāyat, *Tarāneh'hā-ye Khayyām* [Songs of Khayyām] (Tehran: Amir Kabir, 1963), p. 86, no. 54, offers this variant:

> At that castle where Bahrām got a goblet
> Deer gave birth there and foxes found peace and quiet
> Bahrām who hunted onager [*gur*] all his life
> Did you see how the grave [*gur*] got Bahrām?

Another variant is presented in 'Ali Dashti, *Dami bā Khayyām* [A Moment with Khayyām], 2d ed. (Tehran:

Amir Kabir, 1969), the standard study in Persian of 'Omar Khayyām. The first edition of Dashti's study has been translated by L. P. Elwell-Sutton in *In Search of Omar Khayyām* (London: Allen & Unwin, 1971), the variant of the quatrain quoted above in translation appearing as no. 7, p. 202.

17. Richard Ettinghausen, "The Boston Hunting Carpet in Historical Perspective," *Boston Museum Journal* 69, nos. 355–356 (1971): 74–75; black and white illustrations 1, 2, 3, 4, 5, and 7 (pp. 35–39, 41) and the color plates on the cover and frontispiece of the journal show this battle royal.

signs symmetrical on the vertical axis, in which sets of riders, prey, and floral elements are in clusters repeated from the bottom to the top of the field in both the left and right halves of the field surface. As one-directional carpets, such Tabriz hunting designs pose furniture problems in room settings because they can be viewed right side up only from one end of the carpet. Given this inconvenience, the fact that such carpets remain popular may be strong evidence for the conservatism of the people who make and use them in their appreciation of the ruler-subject relations that the monarchical design elements imply. Actually, however, it was not important that persons around classical antique carpets with Safavid hunting and animal patterns view the carpet right side up in terms of design. For example, the famous Safavid Emperor carpet depicts animals that can be seen right side up only from the medallion area—the area in which the king might actually sit or stand in a monumental carpet.[18] As he turned around and observed the design of the carpet, the animal figures would appear right side up from his vantage point. But from anywhere else on the carpet or from beyond the carpet's surface, anyone else would see many figures upside down. Orientation of the design according to the location of the king was another feature of the special place of the king in the order of things. Everyone else had a lesser place and a less complete, accurate, or pleasing view. Of course, in the case of carpets actually intended for royal use, the borders served as a wall or barrier that no one could cross without permission from the royal personage. With such permission, one could enter the royal game preserve, hunting fields, or enclosed royal garden woven into the floor covering and join the king. None of these factors, true of audience-hall size carpets, pertains to smaller modern versions. But the royal associations in the design elements themselves may still obtain.

As with popular hunting carpet designs, few Iranians are consciously aware of the special importance that the highly rational, formal, and idealistic patterns used in the representation of floral forms have in their own impression of beauty in contemporary Persian carpets. Regardless, even if awareness of these design features operates only at the level of comfortable or natural, familiar or

Figure 28. Tabriz hunting scene carpet.

traditional visual appurtenances, these features have a sort of meaning, although it is perhaps somewhat short of symbolic meaning. Further, there is the arguable implication that until the day when Persian carpet designs exhibit essential changes, those traditional cultural values embodied in popular contemporary designs are somehow still relevant to the Iranians who use and treasure the carpets.

The Islamic Vision

Many motifs themselves, their manner of representation, their overall content, and the pattern of many Safavid carpets are evidently symbolic.[19] Many modern Persian carpet patterns designed with an appreciation of the traditions from which they derive seem therefore potentially symbolic. If they are symbolic or at least if they appear to many Iranians today as natural and comfortable features of the visual environment, essential aspects of the Safavid world view represented in the rugs are presumably still relevant to life in Iran.

As for the potential symbolism of Persian carpet patterns as a whole, an obvious starting point

---

18. Ford, *The Oriental Carpet*, p. 81, Plate 178; p. 43, Plate 68 (detail); Erwin Gans-Ruedin, *The Splendor of Persian Carpets*, pp. 64–65.

19. According to Schuyler Cammann, "The Interplay of Art, Literature and Religion in Safavid Symbolism," *Journal of the Royal Asian Society* (1978), p. 124: "The basic pattern of a typical Safavid carpet . . . may appear to represent either an earthly garden or hunting park, or else a view of Paradise; but in most cases, the last seems to have been the original intention of the designer."

can be the maintenance of those aspects of carpet patterns for which there seems to be no reason except convention. For example, the traditional division of design elements on Persian carpets into border and field areas is often viewed as the mere framing of the field pattern by border material that in addition serves as a transition to the space beyond the carpet. According to *Encyclopaedia Britannica*, the border "serves, like the cornice on a building or the frame on a picture, to emphasize the limits, isolate the field, and sometimes control the implied movements of the interior pattern."[20]

But such a view fails to take into account differences between border and field areas in terms of motifs and patterning in many Persian carpets and may be the imposition of a Western conception of framing upon a visual art form to which the concept may not always apply. On many carpets, continuing a tradition dating back at least to thirteenth-century Turkish carpets, "the border creates a frame round a little detail of the infinite that is following on freely without beginning or end. The way the border cuts through single motifs of the central field implies that the field is imagined as endless."[21] Many modern Persian carpets exhibit this representation of infinity. Examples include many Torkaman *gol* carpets (see Fig. 11), Esfahān and Tabriz garden scene carpets, Kāshān *afshān* field carpets (see Fig. 33), and Ardabil Shrine design carpets (see Figs. 37, 38). Other types that exhibit this infinity are the Varāmin carpet with the *minā khāni* pattern (see Fig. 18), Kurdish and other carpets with the *herāti* pattern (see Fig. 17), the Arāk carpet with the *boteh* pattern, and numerous carpets of varied provenance that feature a central medallion with or without corner elements in a field of *shāh 'abbāsi* motifs, vines, leaves, and/or arabesques (see Figs. 4, 5, 29).[22] In each of them, the field pattern does not stop neatly at the border, but seems instead to run on

under and beyond it, as though it could continue on forever, with the border merely isolating this particular section. Not all Persian carpets exhibit this imaginary endlessness, but that many do is sufficient reason not to suppose that Persian carpet borders function as picture frames. Paintings traditionally isolate and bring into focus, through perspective and arrangement of objects, a foreground and central shapes, effecting in the viewer the sense that what the frame encloses is all that there is to see or all that the eye can focus on, usually with no invitation to the viewer to imagine anything beyond the frame. But Persian carpets which feature field elements that are cut off at the borders and seem therefore to run on beneath them do not present a foregrounded view of field material put in any perspective. In fact, in these carpets the border is itself the foreground, the field depicting merely a part of a limitless vision behind or beyond the border.

An example of the failure to visualize the endlessness of the field pattern occurs when a carpet customer or viewer complains, usually about a tribal carpet such as a Baluch *gol* carpet, that the field lacks symmetry because the border has cut off more or less of a particular design element at one edge than another.[23] A typical reaction on the part of an Iranian merchant, seen by the customer as a ploy, is either a shrug of the shoulders as if the point were not really understood, a casual observation that nomads cannot be expected to produce perfectly symmetrical carpets, or an explanation that tribal weavers purposely include errors in their weaving so as not to seem to compete with God through an attempt to create something perfect. But if in such cases the weaver has subconsciously felt comfortable with the border as a window cutting off and framing a slice of infinity and the viewer perceives the pattern in the same terms, the question of "symmetry" becomes irrelevant. In any case, field asymmetry is a conventional feature of Star Ushāk carpet patterns, an important pre-modern Turkish carpet type exhibiting formality and exactitude that preclude a supposition of carelessness on the part of designers or weavers.[24]

As for the significance of these attempts to de-

20. "Rugs and Carpets," *Encyclopaedia Britannica*, 15th ed. (1974).

21. Hübel, *The Book of Carpets*, p. 21; Kurt Erdmann, *Oriental Carpets*, p. 35.

22. Illustrations of classical antique Persian carpets exhibiting such infinity appear in Gans-Ruedin, *The Splendor of Persian Carpets*, p. 35 (Milan hunting carpet), p. 36 (Chelsea carpet), p. 39 (Ardabil Shrine carpet), p. 42 (Anhalt medallion and arabesque carpet), p. 47 (Vienna multiple medallion carpet), p. 56 (medallion and animal carpet at National Gallery, Washington, D.C.). For numerous illustrations of contemporary carpets exhibiting this field infinity, see Ford, *The Oriental Carpet*.

23. An example of a typical modern Baluch carpet with an asymmetrical arrangement of primary and secondary *gol* motifs in its field appears in Ford, *The Oriental Carpet*, p. 194, Plate 434.

24. Ian Bennett, *Complete Illustrated Rugs and Carpets of the World*, p. 106; Daniel S. Walker, *Oriental Rugs of the Hajji Babas*, p. 35, Plate 1.

pict infinity, Islamic art historians declare that it is "connected with the basic concepts of Islamic thought on the infinity of all true being and on the nothingness of all temporary existence," which is to say the infinity of Allāh and spiritual reality.[25] Whether or not the representation of infinity is "a true textile pattern,"[26] it is a very obvious feature of Islamic religious architecture in Iran. For example, both interior and exterior domes often embody patterns that disappear behind and beneath the bands at the bottom of the dome. The Jāme' Mosque in Yazd and the Shrine Mosque in Qom are two examples of domes with geometric, rectilinear infinite patterns. Exhibiting floral, curvilinear infinite patterns are the exterior domes of Shirāz's Shāh Cherāgh Mosque and the Shāh Mosque in Esfahān. The interior dome of the Shaykh Lotfollāh Mosque in Esfahān is a familiar example of a representation of infinity. Moreover, of course, the patterns on the concave or convex dome surfaces prove as the eye circles around to be literally unending.

A second concept which can be related to Moslem architectural decoration and is recognizable in many traditional Persian carpet field patterns is the use of many design elements which compete for attention through size, coloring, or movement.[27] The eye is drawn from one element to another, back again to the medallion if there is one and then away from it to the corners, to one element of an arrangement of *shāh 'abbāsi* motifs, then along vines and tendrils to another. The eye does not rest on any particular element of design surface or shape, including the background color of the field, for long. Nor can the observer ultimately conclude that any one specific motif or locus in the carpet is its most important or significant.

An apparent exception to this contention is the

Figure 29. Nā'in medallion and floral field with animals carpet.

popular Kermān carpet with its field of a solid color in the middle of which appears a medallion, because attention naturally focuses on the bold medallion. (See Fig. 9.) It may also seem an exception in that it does not depict a section of infinity, since few typical Kermāns have corner elements that literally are cut off at and by the border. The modern Kermān design owes its original inspiration not to the adaptation of religious architectural decoration by carpet designers and weavers, but rather to the transfer of book cover and page decoration to the carpet medium during the early Safavid period; consequently, it is natural for the typical Kermān carpet not to represent infinity and indefinability as many other carpet types do. Still, the most pleasing Kermān carpets are those in which the expanse of rich field color balances the floral medallion.

The creation of a sense of equilibrium or balance by the design elements in the field patterns occurs in most carpets with repeat patterns, such as *herāti*, *boteh*, *minā khāni*, and various Torkaman *gol* motifs. Likewise, the medallion and *afshān* carpet patterns which feature *shah 'ab-*

25. Ernst J. Grube, "The Joseph V. McMullan Collection of Islamic Carpets," in *Islamic Carpets* (New York: Near Eastern Research Center, 1965), p. 13.

26. Ibid., p. 12. Oktay Aslanapa, "Seljuk and Ottoman Carpets," *Turkish Art and Architecture*, p. 299, asserts that traditional Turkish carpets are superior to curvilinear Persian designs because they "remained faithful to the laws of textile manufacture" and "rejected any close connection with the art of the book."

27. David James, *Islamic Art: An Introduction* (London: Hamlyn, 1974), p. 66, says of the *mehrāb* of the Jāme' Mosque in Kermān, "Decoration such as this, particularly when covering an entire interior, was designed to create a mood of perfect equilibrium by not allowing the eye to fix on any single point."

bāsi motifs linked with arabesques, the Caucasus-inspired Ardabil and Meshkinshahr multiple medallion carpets (see Fig. 19), Afshār, Qashqā'i, and Khamseh carpets which have rosette and other floral scatter inside and outside the basic polygon which defines much of the field area (see Fig. 34), and various compartment carpets (see Figs. 21, 22, 23) all create a sense of balance, equilibrium, and indefinability of focus. Such is even an effect of the traditional Heris carpet with its impression of superimposed and intersecting field polygons (see Fig. 14).

Further, the creation of the sort of balance found in these carpets involves what Islamic art historians call "the dissolution of matter," an approach to decoration in Islamic architecture originally, whereby solid surfaces are dissolved as it were by filling the whole surface with smaller and smaller decorative units and motifs "to reflect the temporary character of all earthly structures and imply thereby the impermanence of human existence."[28] At the same time, the specific design elements that create this sense of dissolution of matter on two-dimensional surfaces are themselves chosen for reasons which are originally religious. In other words, the predominance in Persian carpets of stylized floral and vegetal forms has to do with the traditional Islamic aversion to the representation of animal forms and human figures.[29] This attitude confronted artists and craftsmen with the problem of representing the physical world symbolically. Consequently the visual arts, calligraphy, book illustrations, architectural decoration, and the other decorative arts which developed in Islamic Iran can be described as abstract, or as the stylization of basic floral and calligraphic patterns. A third way to interpret these arts is as "the denaturalization of nature,"[30] a theme which, along with infinity and indefinability, is common in many modern Persian carpets. These carpets either completely lack figural forms or so stylize them as to make identification difficult or insignificant.

All of this argues for the intimate connections between modern Persian carpet designs and Islamic architectural decoration and for the association of the former with religious notions and values because the same design elements and patterns, when part of the latter, are naturally religious. The many varieties of Persian prayer carpets, whether of tribal, village, or urban origin, are a graphic illustration of these connections; understanding these rugs is a first step toward appreciation of the comprehensive symbolic message which many traditional Persian carpet designs embody.[31]

Prayer carpets, as described in Chapter 3, exhibit a *mehrāb* shape in the upper part of their one-directional field. They are intended for use during ritual prayer incumbent upon Iranian Shi'i Moslems three times a day. The call to prayer by the muezzin in the minaret begins with *allāho akbar*, which literally means "God is greater." In other words, God is greater and more important than anything one may be doing or about which one may be thinking. Therefore, all less important activity should cease and Allāh's greatness acknowledged through prayer. In addition to including a *mehrāb*, many prayer carpets from Kāshān and Qom, among others, depict a sort of gateway, sometimes with a garden beyond to which the viewer seems invited.[32] (See Figs. 25, 26.)

Throughout the Koran, Allāh promises "the believers, men and women, gardens underneath which rivers flow, forever therein to dwell, and goodly dwelling-places in the Gardens of Eden." Therefore, the garden imagery of the prayer carpet should remind the believer of the garden of heaven as described in the Koran as the reward

---

28. Grube, *The World of Islam*, pp. 12–17; see also Cammann, "Symbolic Meanings," p. 17.

29. Oleg Grabar, *The Formation of Islamic Art* (New Haven, Conn.: Yale University Press, 1973), pp. 75–103.

30. Cammann, "Symbolic Meanings," p. 11.

31. According to Arthur Upham Pope, *Persian Architecture*, p. 9, in traditional Iranian architecture the "guiding, formative motif was cosmic symbolism by which man was brought into communication and participation with the powers of Heaven."

32. According to Cammann, "Symbolic Meanings," pp. 17–21: "The key to the deeper meaning of the arch-shaped device on the rugs and the arch surrounding the *mehrāb* in a mosque, or the *mehrāb* itself, is that each of these stood for a gateway . . . the concept of a gate has always taken a special prominence in the Islamic cultures . . . The arch design, then, could symbolize the Gate of Prayer, or the Gate to Paradise in Inmost Heaven beyond the Sky Door . . ." Oleg Grabar, *Islamic Architecture and Its Decoration, A.D. 800–1500* (Chicago: University of Chicago Press, 1964), pp. 77–79, cites similarities between the *mehrāb* and a gate in terms of the development of decoration in and around each as well as in terms of "basic features . . . such as a central void, side walls, and a rectangular frame." However, he mentions only the *mehrāb* and not the gate "as the inspiration for decorative designs on . . . prayer rugs." Further, there seems to be nothing in the denotations or etymology of the word *mehrāb* to suggest "gate" or "gateway."

of "those who believe and do deeds of righteousness," "the god-fearing" people, "God's sincere servants." Chief among such "deeds of righteousness" are the daily ritual prayers for which the prayer carpet is intended.[33]

Other obviously religious carpets are those of varied provenance that depict in their fields adaptations of the entire decorative structure of the interior of mosque domes, notably those of the Shaykh Lotfollāh and Shāh mosques in Esfahān.[34] Similarly, there are carpets of varied provenance that copy the patterns of Safavid carpets which were intended for a specific religious setting, such as the famous pair of sixteenth-century carpets presumably used at the Shaykh Safiyoddin Shrine in Ardabil. The latter feature representations of mosque lamps on the vertical axis of the field, and their central medallions seem to be reflections of the dome medallions of mosque interiors. This Ardabil Shrine pattern appears in contemporary carpets from Kāshān, Mashhad, Tabriz, Tehrān, and other weaving centers. (See Figs. 37, 38.) The Ardabil Shrine design is discussed in detail at the end of Chapter 5.

In light of the connections between carpet designs and religious architectural decoration, one answer to the question of what some carpet patterns may symbolize involves appreciation of the symbolism in the religious architectural decoration that has inspired many carpet designs. At the very least, the fact that the designs on both surfaces are the same and that the latter is holy makes the former holy by extension.

Because mosques, their courtyards, and minarets never include statuary, painted scenes of human figures, or anything that might strike a Westerner as exclusively religious iconography, the symbolism found in Islamic religious architecture may be difficult to discern at first for observers who expect to find more representational symbolism. Nonetheless, the symbolism is there. First, the mosque entranceway or portal, often

with minarets paired on either side, invites the worshiper; it becomes a gateway, as it were, to salvation. Second, insofar as salvation involves the creature's future life in heaven, the iconography of the mosque portal and dome surfaces is heavenly. There may be sky colors, star and sun shapes, the curved surface that strikes the eye as the physical sky does from horizon to horizon. The mosque dome brings heaven down to earth so that the worshiper might contemplate it. The visual message is for the worshiper to appreciate this vision of salvation and behave accordingly in order to gain entrance to the real heavenly paradise after death.[35]

A third feature of Islamic religious architectural decoration that is replicated in the traditional designs of many modern Persian carpets is the image of heaven or paradise as a perfect garden. Arabesques, vines, leaves, *shāh 'abbāsi* motifs, and other stylized vegetal and floral shapes occur repeatedly in Islamic architectural decoration in Iran. The mosque surface and grounds become, therefore, a visual glimpse of the heavenly garden paradise that the Koran promises true believers.[36] Fourth, as if to instantiate the symbolic content of the vegetal, floral, stellate, and sunburst decoration, the word "Allāh" and the literal words of God as recorded in the Koran in Arabic are incorporated into the decorative structure of portals, dome bands, minaret cylinders, and the like. Even the illiterate Moslem can contemplate Allāh and His words by gazing at the depiction of heaven which is accompanied by often ornate calligraphy. On the basis of inscriptions, poems, and other literary evidence, not to speak of the contextual evidence offered by car-

---

33. The most readable translation is Arthur J. Arberry's *The Koran Interpreted* (Boston: Allen & Unwin, 1980; first published in 1964), 367 pp.
34. Simin Dāneshvar and Gertrude Nye Dorry, *Persian Carpet Appreciation*, Plate 123. In the Introduction, p. 5, "Patterns of Historic Monuments and Islamic Buildings" is cited as a major design classification of Persian carpets. Besides the Shaykh Lotfollāh Mosque, the following Islamic buildings are also cited as having inspired carpet designs: Esfahān's Shāh Mosque, Tabriz's Blue Mosque, and the Shaykh Safiyoddin Shrine in Ardabil.

35. L. V. Golombek, "Anatomy of a Mosque," in *Iranian Civilization and Culture*, ed. Charles J. Adams, p. 10, sees the mosque portal as a "gateway to salvation," with inscriptions at the Shāh Mosque including the Prophet's invitation to the faithful to "come to the gate," the whole mosque constituting "a preview of paradise, a splendid garden."
36. According to Maurice S. Dimand, *Oriental Rugs in the Metropolitan Museum of Art*, pp. 40–41: "To the Persians of the Safavid period such designs [i.e., floral and animal-floral] suggested gardens. The verses that appear in a number of Safavid rugs confirm this, those of [one] rug reading in part, 'This is no carpet, but a wild white rose . . . a garden full of tulips and roses.'" Speaking of early Safavid medallion carpets, Erdmann, *Oriental Carpets*, p. 33, observes: "The carpet turns into a landscape . . . Here the garden concept has indeed expanded—the carpet has become a portrayal of paradise itself."

pets themselves from Safavid formal garden carpets down to contemporary Bakhtiyārī garden compartment and Torkaman *gol* carpets, it is obvious that many modern Persian carpets depict an idealized garden, an earthly or heavenly paradise.

The representation of infinity and the dissolution of matter in both religious architectural decoration and traditional carpet designs persuade the observer of the religious nature of the motifs and patterns found in those carpets. For example, as one Islamic art historian puts it: "The spiritual, contemplative quality of an arabesque pattern is always there in potential." Or ". . . because floral forms, which were an important part of the [mosque] decoration, had distinct associations with Paradise, the believer could be brought to contemplate the goal of existence."[37] Important calligraphic evidence indicating symbolic intent is woven into dozens of Safavid floral carpets. Verses appearing in the borders of these carpets describe the springtime beauties of nature and the garden pleasures of paradise as depicted in the carpets' designs.[38]

Another sort of textual evidence for the appreciation of these traditional Persian carpet designs in religiously symbolic terms is presented in an anonymous early-sixteenth-century Persian poem on the subject of a Safavid garden carpet. The poem begins with the observation that in the carpet which the speaker observes and describes lives an eternal spring unaffected by summer heat, autumn storms, or winter cold.

The carpet's border is described as a garden wall protecting the park within it. That park is an enchanting setting for solitude, conversation, music, celebrations, and lovers. The carpet's field area is described as a place to rest eyes irritated by the sun's glare, sore limbs wearied by the desert's rigors, and tired hearts.

In contrast to the haven and security which the garden carpet provides, the world beyond it is described as full of peril and death.

The poetic speaker then observes that earthly gardens are naturally transient, but not so the fadeless garden of heavenly paradise which awaits pilgrim humans who deserve its rewards. The garden carpet reminds the observer of heavenly paradise, the speaker continues, as do hand-

drawn and hand-painted book covers and page decorations. The garden carpet is a "token and counterpart" of the garden of paradise. It is "Heaven's glory brought more nigh: / An assurance and a prophecy."

The speaker then describes the carpet's design elements. There are flower buds, blossoms, flowers of many sorts, vines, tendrils, all of them with a vitality that seems to represent "the heartbeat of God." The central medallion is described as "the all-powerful sun, / A golden lion commanding the skies," stirring creation below by its "life-giving power" which "flows down through the cosmic axis."

The speaker concludes his paean to the beautiful garden carpet by asserting that the carpet's perfect proportions and harmony that are integrated into a transcendent unity can reveal to the observer the mind of God, God being the ultimate goal and answer. The speaker says:

From snares of self set free,
In august and tranquil beauty
At last we see the beloved's face,
And there attain our journey's end,
Our life's reward and final destiny—
Refuge and fulfillment in His Infinity.[39]

Whether one argues from such literary evidence as this poem or from either demonstrable symbolic intent in Irano-Islamic architectural decoration or the contextual evidence of many Persian carpets themselves, it seems reasonable to hold that many traditional patterns depicted in modern Persian carpets exhibit the significance and symbolism described in this chapter. At the very least, the depiction of vegetal and floral elements in the fields of almost all sorts of modern Persian carpets represents an Iranian vision of the ideal physical environment, either springtime or

---

37. James, *Islamic Art*, p. 57.

38. Dimand, *Oriental Rugs in the Metropolitan*, pp. 40–41; Ian Bennett, ed., *Complete Illustrated Rugs and Carpets of the World*, pp. 70 ff.

39. "Ode to a Garden Carpet," in Arthur Upham Pope et al., *A Survey of Persian Art from Prehistoric Times to the Present*, vol. 14, pp. 3184–3186. The summary here is an informal prose paraphrase of Pope's verse translation. The Persian original was unavailable. The significance of spring, gardens, and paradise imagery in Persian culture has been much studied: e.g., William L. Hanaway, Jr., "Paradise on Earth: The Terrestrial Garden in Persian Literature," in *The Islamic Garden*, ed. Elizabeth B. MacDougall and Richard Ettinghausen (Washington, D.C.: Dumbarton Oaks, Trustees for Harvard University, 1976), pp. 41–67; Elizabeth B. Moynihan, *Paradise as a Garden: In Persia and Mughal India* (New York: George Braziller, 1978); and Donald L. Wilber, *Persian Gardens and Garden Pavilions* (Rutland, Vt.: Charles E. Tuttle, 1962).

paradise, the perfect garden or Eden or the Islamic heaven.

If traditional field patterns on modern Persian carpets are interpreted as depictions of paradise, the border pattern takes on further symbolic meaning. The whole carpet, border and field, sometimes represents a "universe in miniature." The infinite and the spiritual are represented in the field, contrasting with the temporal symbolized in the border by "bold, repeating motifs" that imply "the orderly progress of time as it proceeds in regularly recurring cycles," sometimes with the suggestion of alternating night and day when motifs alternating within the border are inverted or when one is darker than the other. What appear to be alternating sun and moon shapes in the border of many Torkaman Tekkeh *gol* carpets (see Fig. 11) seem a good example of a border area's representing the physical world while the field symbolizes Allāh's paradise beyond this world. The border represents, as it were, a door through the physical sky or heaven to the spiritual heaven beyond it.[40]

While the central medallions of some traditional Persian carpet types do not seem to be part of the paradise garden constituted by the floral decoration in the field, their shapes could be interpreted as suns or stars (as suggested in the Safavid poem paraphrased above) and hence as part of the celestial garden or paradise such carpets depict. These shapes might also represent distant heavens beyond the sky of the human world as represented by the main border of the carpet. These distant heavens could be layers of paradise, perhaps implying that God's abode or throne is situated beyond the farthest sun or star. This latter speculation has been called the "sungate" concept.[41] While speculation of this sort is interesting, one may conservatively suppose that such medallion shapes are often heavenly garden elements and no more, since these sun and stellate shapes from seventeenth-century Star Ushak design Turkish carpets down to contemporary multiple medallion Karājeh carpets have constituent vegetal and floral elements.

All of the above attributions of symbolic significance to design features of modern Persian carpets need to be weighed against at least one undeniable fact. Few Iranians consciously reflect on the designs of their own carpets in such terms.

In fact, there are almost no references to symbolism in modern Persian carpet designs to be found in the literature written in the Persian language on carpets. On the other hand, there was an official Pahlavi government position on the matter during the latter years of its support for specific aspects of Iranian culture. For example, the foreword to the Pahlavi-subsidized *Splendor of Persian Carpets* (1978) reads in part: "On the creative and aesthetic level, the hope of reaching the Garden of Paradise, a nostalgic aspiration that has developed in harmony with Iranian philosophy and spirituality, has become a reality in the interlaced forms and in the beauty of our carpets. This enchanted garden has led man, ever since the Sāsānian era, towards an ideal conception of beauty and freshness."[42]

Furthermore, some contemporary Iranian writers and other intellectuals attach considerable cultural significance to Persian carpets. A good example is M. E. Beh'āzin (b. 1915), who has a brief piece called "The Carpet of Iran" in *Designs in Silk*, a 1956 collection of prose sketches and reminiscences. It reads:

O suffering and beautiful and forbearing soul of my country, O splendid design of the carpet of Iran!

In the details of the apparently agitated order of your design, in the twists and turns of your imagination-inciting branches and leaves, in the colors of the splendor of the harvest of your flowers, I once again found my Iran. You better than anything else have grafted me to the distant past of the homeland. You made me aware of the long road my ancestors traveled along. In you I visualize the efforts and struggling of the centuries. God forbid that my gaze should tire of looking at you. The intoxicated smile over your decorated expanse is blended with sighs and tears. The heart-warming freshness of your countenance draws a curtain over the perplexity of suffering and unfulfilled desires. The silent melodies of your profusion of warps and wefts seem to be a tune of the sorrow and injustice of our times that gives news of a joyous future. You are the well-spring of the birth of eternal designs and colors, a new immortality and change. You are our suffering, our love, our hope, our life. You are the soul of Iran!

O suffering and beautiful and forbearing soul of my country, I kiss your design that has been cleansed with blood and tears. Each time I see you my eyes acquire light, a bubbling strength comes to me, my stature truly becomes more grand. I stride with pride, yet I'm not for a moment without regret that sometimes with

40. Cammann, "Symbolic Meanings," p. 14.
41. Ibid.

42. Gans-Ruedin, *The Splendor of Persian Carpets*, p. 5.

the feet of what terrible people you must be stepped on! . . .[43]

To put the symbolism of Persian carpet designs discussed in this chapter into a context familiar to most readers, one might without undue exaggeration suppose that Mohammad Rezā Shāh Pahlavi (reigned 1941–1979) had only to look down at his feet to realize that the Iran he presumed to lead toward secular modernization was at the core a society attached to and most at home with a traditional Shi'i Islamic world view, with its infinite Allāh, the promise of Paradise, and the message that this material world and transient human existence were not to be valued too highly. Further, the existence of such great variety in modern Persian carpet patterns might have served as a warning to the Pahlavi regime against attempting to homogenize the various Iranian peoples. Although the Iranian government was referred to as a *shāhanshāhi* [empire] and its leader as *shāhanshāh* [emperor] during the Pahlavi era, the government did not behave in the traditional imperial Iranian fashion. Doing so would have required a federal system that would probably have managed Baluch, Torkaman, Āzarbāyjān, Kurdish, and other areas whose populations were not inclined to submit to the imposition of Persian Iranian culture more efficiently than could the increasingly centralized government. A traditional Iranian emperor would have

43. Mahmud E'temādzādeh Beh'āzin, "Qāli-ye Iran" [Carpet of Iran], in *Naqsh-e Parand* [Design in Silk] (Tehrān: Nil, 1956), pp. 56–57 (my translation).

given such non-Persian Iranian peoples some cultural and linguistic autonomy, a possibility which the Pahlavi policy of Persification did not allow.

On the other hand, the leaders of the Islamic Republic of Iran that Ruhollāh Khomayni brought into power in 1979 need only reflect on those very same carpets to recognize that Iran is not a monolith of devout Shi'i Moslems. Iranianness also includes certain essentially non-Islamic elements. Many Iranians have been comfortable with the sort of ruler-subject relations and the ceremonial, ritual aspects of social intercourse fostered by traditional monarchy, not to speak of the pleasures of social intercourse and aspects of hospitality which Persian carpets as furniture represent. It is, parenthetically, ironic that many of the carpets woven in the religious city of Qom exhibit intimate secular and royalist associations. Specifically, the smaller *afshān*, arabesque, and stellate medallion carpets and other carpets exhibiting *shāh 'abbāsi* motifs and other curvilinear elements in field and border areas are heirs to the design traditions originally commissioned by Safavid monarchs. The Khomayni regime might further recognize the message to be found in traditional carpet designs, which represent a subordination of religion to political forces as a natural relationship in Iranian society. Finally, the fact of great Western influence in motifs and colors of popular Kermān and Arāk medallion carpets might serve as symbolic evidence that Iranian culture has ever been an adaptive, assimilating force, which a xenophobic, isolationist government can presumably not stifle permanently.

5. Persian Carpets and Iranian Society

During the heyday of the Pahlavi monarchy in the early 1970s, Westerners acquainted with Iran would have had little difficulty recognizing the connections between Persian carpet designs and Iranian monarchy. Besides connections described under "The Lion, the Hunt, and Royal Themes" in Chapter 4, there are other interesting associations. Persian carpets were Mohammad Rezā Shāh Pahlavi's inevitable gifts to foreign heads of state and underfoot at almost all official events. Special attention was given during the later Pahlavi years to the Iranian carpet industry through "the allocation of funds for the establishment of carpet-weaving factories in different regions of the country, in the course of which a reported 12,000 new carpet weavers were trained, and the industry was introduced to some regions where it had not existed before." Then, with government controls, there was subsequent emphasis on "the quality aspect of carpet production and export promotion."[1] The Pahlavi government, in fact, entered the carpet business through the Iran Carpet Company. It had a retail outlet on Tehrān's Ferdowsi Street, the world's largest carpet retail location with its then 150 or more stores.[2]

The final events of Pahlavi involvement with Persian carpets were the opening of the Carpet Museum of Iran in Tehrān in late 1977 and the publication of Erwin Gans-Ruedin's *The Splendor of Persian Carpets* (1978), in part a pictorial record of the Carpet Museum of Iran collection.[3]

From the post-Pahlavi vantage point of the 1980s, the grandeur of the museum, the lavishness of *The Splendor of Persian Carpets*, and the monumental Esfahān carpet commissioned in the mid-1970s by the monarch for the Parliament Building[4] exemplify one sort of unrealism of the Pahlavi regime. The monarchy persisted in sponsoring projects that could only further antagonize those Iranians whose exploitation over the centuries is documented implicitly by the museum, *The Splendor of Persian Carpets*, and many monumental city carpets.

In one sense, this situation highlights a basic but unpleasant truth. From shepherd to weaver to merchant, Persian carpets are testimony to a most unromantic, traditional fact of such a handicraft in Iranian life: the exploitation of illiterate, unskilled masses. Most of the million or so Iranians involved in carpet production have always been poor. They are the anonymous Iranians who have been doing the physical labor of those Iranians with recorded names associated with royal courts since construction began at Persepolis nearly 2,500 years ago. Whatever else Persian carpets are shown to signify, as long as they are in abundance, one can guess that the bulk of Iranian society is just barely surviving economically. This fact was an ever-present part of the monarchical heritage until its demise in early 1979. The irony, of course, is that there is no denying that these same Persian carpets are true, pleasurable, and sometimes superlative artistic statements of an idealistic sort about a society whose people, by and large, have extremely difficult lives.

1. C.P., "An Old Look for New Carpets," *Tehran Journal* (May 27, 1975), p. 5, reports the Iran Carpet Company's achievements in research, carpet design, publications, and expansion of the weaving industry and export market during the early 1970s.

2. The Iran Carpet Company sponsored the publication of Simin Dāneshvar and Gertrude Nye Dorry's *Masterpieces of Persian Carpet* (1973) and *Persian Carpet Appreciation* (1974), which featured two hundred color plates of carpet designs being produced by the ICC.

3. The opening of the Carpet Museum of Iran was

reported by Siawosch Azadı in *Hali* 1 (1978): 45, the journal itself espousing a royalist position during that tumultuous year in Iran. Erwin Gans-Ruedin's *Splendor of Persian Carpets* was published in conjunction with the museum's opening.

4. See the first paragraph in Chapter 3.

From a pre-1978 perspective, Westerners familiar with Iran would have probably felt that "the Islamic vision" described in Chapter 4 as the essential message of Persian carpets was abstract cultural content or the comfortable vestige of a religious era gone by, rather than a clue that the real cement that held Iran together sociologically was religious and that the outlook of most Iranians, whether tribal, rural, or urban, was essentially religious. The message was there in Persian carpet designs. But it took the civil upheaval that began in Iran in 1978 to make the vital, intimate connections between religious elements in carpet designs and the basic fabric of Iranian life obvious once again. As it turned out, the very people whose economically marginal lives have revolved around Persian carpet-weaving for generations were the people who genuinely supported not merely the fall of the Pahlavi monarchy, but more importantly the establishment of the Islamic Republic of Iran.

By the time *The Splendor of Persian Carpets* was published in mid-1978, the Pahlavi monarchy was already doomed. By the mid-1980s, with the Islamic Republic of Iran firmly in place as a successor regime, only a few Ferdowsi Street shops remained open in what had been for decades the largest concentration of retail shops in the world. Their foreign customers had all but disappeared, and their mostly Jewish Iranian owners were mostly in Israel and Los Angeles.

This change does not mean a diminution of the significance of Persian carpets in Iranian life. Although carpet exports decreased substantially from 1979 into the mid-1980s, production seems not to have decreased much during the first five years of the Islamic Republic. In fact, more of the less finely woven, everyday carpets are being produced as more and more women, no longer able to enter the labor force as readily as during the Pahlavi era, began supplementing family income in towns and cities through carpet-weaving, an important domestic craft in Qom even during the Pahlavi era because women in that religious center were less likely than other Iranian women to have jobs outside the home. In addition, the function of Persian carpets in public life and official places has been in no way reduced with the overthrow of a monarchical system by a theocratic political organization. On mosque floors, underfoot during prayers, in reception halls and rooms, Persian carpets remain ubiquitous in Iran. (The Carpet Museum of Iran was still in operation in the mid-1980s.)

The sanctions that Western nations placed on Iran in the early 1980s, different sorts of foreign control over Iranian assets outside the country, the manifold effects of the Iran-Iraq War, the problems in the oil and transportation industries, and the great flight of private capital along with many of Iran's most educated and wealthy citizens from Iran to the West, among other problems, created astronomic inflation in Iran during the early 1980s. Accompanying this was great uncertainty among the middle class about their financial future and mistrust of banks and real estate investments. Many Iranians were turning by 1982 to the purchase of carpets for investment, resulting in the unprecedented situation of Persian carpets in some areas retailing for higher prices in Tehrān than in Europe. Despite soaring prices, Iranians realized that Persian carpets were a secure investment that, even if purchased at an artificially inflated price, would someday appreciate to a point beyond what might be expected of any other sort of investment.

The continued appeal of the Persian carpet for Iranians of various classes may also be evidence of their wish to maintain ties with their traditions through the traditional features of carpets, namely their designs. Throughout this book, whatever meaning Persian carpet designs are assumed to embody has to do with their being a conservative art form, as designs that share essential characteristics. Their colorfulness, rational plan, and order are responses to the general physical environment that lacks those qualities. Their common vocabulary of *shāh 'abbāsi* motifs, floral medallions, and the like is linked with traditional Iranian monarchy. Aspects of infinity, indefinability, dissolution of matter, and denaturalization of nature are reflections of a traditional Islamic world view. Taken as a whole, as a design medium with conservative tendencies, Persian carpets depict in an exciting and pleasing way earthly and heavenly paradise.

Variety in Persian Carpet Designs

As has been stated in several contexts, Persian carpets are characterized by great variety that is as significant as what individual carpets have in common. This great contemporary variety in Persian carpet designs and patterns is evidence for a number of observations about Iranian society.

First, it is testimony to the remarkable diversity and rate of change in nearly all aspects of

Figure 30. One-hundredth anniversary commemorative of Iranian postage stamps. Issued by the Pahlavi monarchy in 1967 in commemoration of a century of production of Iranian postage stamps, this stamp intimates how much a part of monarchical Iran curvilinear carpet patterns were. The very outline of the stamp exhibits floral and vegetal material, alternation of motifs, and continuity of movement around the rectangular surface that have been characteristic of curvilinear Persian carpets for four centuries. The replication of the first Iranian postage stamp is also significant in these terms, since it illustrates the familiar quincunx field arrangement of medallion carpets: the lion in the central circle and the four smaller circles containing the Arabic numeral in the corners.

Figure 31. Islamic Republic of Iran "Persian rug" stamp. Called "Persian Rug" in the *Stanley Gibbons Stamp Catalogue*, Part 16 (1981): 101, this 1979 Iranian postage stamp was one of the first and most-printed issues during the first year of the Islamic Republic of Iran. Its pattern is reminiscent of the quincunx arrangement of Iran's first postage stamp commemorated in a 1967 Pahlavi era stamp illustrated in Figure 30 with the Arabic numeral and *riyal* denomination in the corners and the words "Islamic Republic of Iran" in Arabic script in the central medallion. In addition, its other design elements demonstrate how compatible curvilinear carpet motifs and floral patterns are to religious elements in Iran. For example, the main border features vines connecting alternating arabesques, and the field features pendants beyond the central medallion on the vertical axis, a vine system with arabesques, and cloud bands.

post–World War II Iran.[5] The variety in Persian carpets during the 1960s and 1970s has reflected diversity of taste and creative impulses among Iranian designers and some weavers as well as great diversity of taste among the Iranian population for whom these carpets are basic furniture.

Second, insofar as carpets have been a relatively expensive yet widely distributed and purchased commodity within Iran, the very activity of the carpet market through the 1960s and 1970s indicated the existence of a large group of Iranians in an economic middle class. Third, the availability of carpets in sufficient numbers and kinds in urban centers throughout the country, the distribution and other marketing problems caused by the civil upheaval commencing in 1978 notwithstanding, is testimony to the existence of organized exploitation of weavers, efficient distribution and marketing, and the development of production centers to meet domestic consumer demand through the 1970s. Fourth, the retail operations in the larger cities, particularly in bazaars and fancy boulevard and hotel shops, signaled the importance of tourism in Iran during the 1960s and most of the 1970s in addition to Iranian awareness of the appeal of carpets to foreign tourists.

Fifth, if tourism was one indication of Pahlavi Iran's openness to the outside world, the diversity in carpet designs and patterns is another. For contemporary Persian carpets clearly exhibit influences of carpets from Central Asia in the Torkaman groups of carpets, the Soviet Union in the Caucasus-inspired carpets of Ardabil, Karājeh, Meshkinshahr, and even Yalameh carpets, and Western Europe and North America in general widening of carpets and muting of colors, as well as in such designs as one sort of Arāk, Bijār, and Kermān floral medallion carpet. Through the later Pahlavi years Iran continued to be a crossroads culture, as it were, with its traditional and distinctive capacity for adaptation and assimilation.

Sixth, the appeal of silk carpets, responsible for

---

5. Karim Emāmi, "Modern Persian Artists," in *Iran Faces the Seventies*, ed. Ehsān Yārshāter (New York: Praeger, 1971), p. 349, observes: "The artistic scene in Iran today is remarkable for the variety and diversity of its trends, a development . . . hardly surprising for a country going through rapid change. . . . The diversity of the art movement has its parallels in the current life of the country. For here, too, we see the same preoccupation with the archaic past and the futuristic present, and the same regular pendulum-like swing between the 'modern' West and the 'ancient' East."

Figure 32. An Iranian child's view of Persian carpet-weaving. Issued in October 1972 as part of an annual Week of the Child commemorative series, this Iranian stamp presents a nine-year-old child's painting of girls weaving a Persian carpet. The choice of the subject and its constituent elements implies the extent of pile carpet-weaving in Iran and the role which exploitation of children and women has played in it even during the later Pahlavi years of modernization programs.

the growth of the industry in Qom and a dimension of carpet production in Nā'in and Esfahān as well, seems indicative of class differences among Iranian buyers. In comparison with a wool carpet, a silk carpet is harder to sit on, colder, less durable, and ultimately less enduring in its reflection of design through color. However, silk is considerably more expensive than wool and has a rich, luxurious appearance and sheen. With these characteristics to recommend it, the Iranian consumer who wishes to communicate his or her affluence might naturally choose a silk carpet.[6]

Seventh, at the other end of the scale of the economics and production of Persian carpets, the continuing high production level of carpets indicates that a giant labor force composed of some children, some men, and many women still exists in both rural and urban communities and remains unchallenged by mechanized industry. This fact means that industrialization in the sense of an infrastructure that might naturally draw to it the bulk of the unskilled labor force may be a long way off in Iran, regardless of the government of the moment. Further, should the Islamic Republic of Iran prove enduring, carpet production in Iran might increase, since Western-influenced industrialization and employment in modern occupations will be less likely to receive the encouragement from the religious establishment that they did from the modernizing Pahlavi regime.

Finally, the growing amount of tribal weaving reaching the marketplace as time passes seems to imply a diminution of nomadism; tribal weaving in excess of domestic needs means weaving for cash because the nomadic cycle may be failing in economic terms.[7]

Glimpses of Iranian Society through Persian Carpets

Consideration of Persian carpets in general terms and of common features of Persian carpets of whatever provenance is one focus for information about Iranian society and culture. The study of individual Persian carpet design types is just as fruitful, as demonstrated in the earlier discussion of social implications of popular Tabriz hunting carpet designs (Chapter 4). As a continuation of that sort of analysis, five very common contemporary Persian carpet types are here discussed specifically in terms of Iranian society. First is a familiar *afshān* field design that has much to say about ceremony, formality, and ritual in Iranian social intercourse. Second is a popular Qashqā'i *boteh* medallion and floral field carpet that reflects significant features of contemporary Iranian tribal life. Third is a *lachak-toranj* (medallion and corner elements) design that is a typical example of the everyday town and city carpet. Fourth is a Baluch tree-of-life prayer carpet illustrating Iranian village attitudes. Fifth is an example of an Ardabil Shrine design carpet that may be the most revealing contemporary design of all.

AFSHĀN DESIGN CARPETS

The word *afshān* means "scattered" in Persian, as stars might be described as scattered throughout the sky. Although the *afshān* pattern may give an initial impression of spontaneity in its arrangement of *shāh 'abbāsi* motifs, leaves, and smaller flowers throughout a field lacking both central medallion and corner elements, the pattern is anything but haphazard or spontaneous. It is a biaxially symmetrical design that communicates calmness, rationality, complexity, formality, and luxuriousness. The *afshān* design appears in carpets of all sizes and of varied provenance. In distinctive colors and weave, they are woven in Tabriz, Esfahān, Qom, and other cities. The classic contemporary *afshān* carpet, which typically features a palette of blues, greys, and cream colors, is woven in Kāshān, a typical medium-sized

6. Roy Macey, "Silk Carpets in the Modern World," *Hali* 1 (1978): 137.

7. Robert Dillon, "Carpet Capitalism and Craft Involution in Kermān," pp. 281–284.

Iranian plateau city southeast of Qom, due east of the main road from Tehrān through Qom to Esfahān. (See Fig. 33.) The Kāshān *afshān* carpet is a typical city carpet, as are the Kermān floral medallion with plain field carpet (see Fig. 9) and the everyday *lachak-toranj* medallion with floral field carpet which features a ground color of relatively bright red and is woven in cities and towns throughout Iran (see Fig. 35).

All three types of floral city carpets have associations with royalty and monarchical traditions as described earlier. All three, insofar as their constituent floral elements both adhere to traditional Islamic iconophobia and reflect floral and vegetal forms equally familiar as prominent elements in Islamic religious architectural decoration, likewise give testimony to the religious essence of social life in Iran, also discussed earlier. All three seem to point to another significant feature of contemporary Iranian society, cited only in passing to this point, but which a closer look at a typical Kāshān *afshān* carpet seems to reveal.

In one of his shorter odes, the Roman poet Horace voices his preference for the simple life with the simple pleasures of wine and communion with nature. It is a common enough theme in various literary traditions, including traditional Persian literature, as in famous quatrains associated with the name of 'Omar Khayyām. But Horace begins his brief poem by stating: "I hate Persian pomp."[8] Six centuries earlier, on a great platform about twenty-five miles northeast of today's Shirāz, beside the road from Shirāz through Ābādeh to Esfahān and Tehrān, Persian Achaemenid monarchs began construction of a great religious shrine called Persepolis in English. Today the most imposing and important ruin on the Iranian plateau, Persepolis gives voice in bas reliefs and in the arrangement of entranceways and halls to pomp, ceremony, and ritual in social intercourse. In short, at least for the ruling classes throughout Iranian history, ceremony, pomp, and ritual have counted for more in Iran than in some neighboring non-Persian societies. The Persianized court of Hārun al-Rashid at Baghdād, Shāh 'Abbās the Great's construction of the Shāh Square in Esfahān, and, more recently, the pomp and pageantry Mohammad Rezā Pahlavi organized for his 1967 coronation and for the 1971 celebration of 2,500 years of monarchy on the Iranian plateau are merely three examples.

But what Horace was talking about and what foreign observers in Iran have observed in Iranian social intercourse for centuries is not a phenomenon exclusively associated with the royal court. There seems to be a distinctive inclination in Persian Iranian culture and society for ceremony, ritual, and demonstration of politeness, deference, and formality. A carpet design such as the *afshān* pattern reflects such tendencies. On the other hand, designs that are Turkic in origin, that is, most traditional rectilinear patterns and such hybrid designs as the combination of rectilinear and curvilinear impulses in medallion patterns from Heris and Hamadān do not seem to communicate such tendencies. (See Figs. 14, 17.)

As a carpet that can be room-size, the *afshān* carpet is often placed in the formal living room or dining room. These rooms more often than not are adjacent and lead from one to another in Iranian homes; they are generally not used except for entertaining guests. Even modern Tehrān apartments are commonly designed with this cultural convention in mind. The apartment or house front door or entranceway opens into a large hall or the equivalent of a family room in which more everyday family activities take place. The bedrooms may be beyond this room through a door that in effect leads to the private part of the house. Another door may lead to the kitchen. Still another leads to the formal living room and dining room, the door(s) of which may even be kept locked to prevent children from messing these rooms up.

The order, formality, and ceremony communicated by an *afshān* carpet as the main carpet in an Iranian living room or dining room are paralleled by the behavior of the occupants of those rooms. Greetings, leave-takings, seating arrangements, the serving of various beverages and fruit before dinner, the dinner itself, and postprandial activity, including conversation, are generally stylized and conventional for Persian Iranian urbanites. There are expected comments to which there are expected replies, literally word-for-word exchanges that occur on occasion after occasion in exactly the same terms and tone. Deferential honorifics, complimentary observations, the maintenance of a social hierarchy in conversation, and numerous other features of social life that can be subsumed under the Persian term *ta'ārof*[9]

---

8. Horace, *Odes*, Book 1, #38, line 1: "Persicos odi, puer, apparatus."

9. For more on the *ta'ārof* system, see Michael Hillmann, "Language and Social Distinctions in Iran," in *Modern Iran: The Dialectics of Continuity and Change*, ed. Michael Bonine and Nikki Keddie (Albany: State University of New York, 1981), pp. 327–340, 438–439.

are a most appropriate set of interaction activities in a setting created by a Kāshān *afshān* carpet.

The dictionary defines the noun *ta'ārof* as "compliment, offer, gift, formality, good manners, honeyed phrases, respect." The verb *ta'ārof kardan* (literally: to make/do *ta'ārof*) is defined as "to use compliments, to stand upon ceremony, to make present of, to speak (with) courtesy." In everyday Persian conversation, Iranians use the term to mean some verbal offer or invitation that one neither literally means nor expects to be accepted, but rather that one intends as a show of respect alone.

The hundreds of set terms, phrases, questions, and responses that constitute the Persian *ta'ārof* system seem to have various purposes. One is simply the expression of cordiality, warmth, and hospitality. A second is the strategic use of deferential terms in talking with others so as to persuade them to fulfill one's requests or to dissuade them from persisting in their own requests. A third function seems to be political. *Ta'ārof* expressions enable one to avoid frank public statement of views or direct involvement in public interaction situations. At the same time one can show obvious and formal respect to others while maintaining self-respect by virtue of appearing cultivated through demonstration of acquaintance with the intricacies of the *ta'ārof* system. This function of the *ta'ārof* system might be labeled its ruler-subject dimension. Symptomatic of it are all of the stylized terms and gestures of respect that literally communicate a relationship as between a servant and a master or between ruled and ruler which even social equals employ with one another in Iranian social intercourse. For example, in everyday conversation, Iranians routinely refer to themselves as "slaves" and to the person they are addressing as "your excellency." Their questions are routinely called "petitions," and expected replies are referred to as "commands." Almost every urban Iranian verbally participates in the ruler-subject patterns of *ta'ārof*, with each individual given more or less frequent opportunities to play the role of the ruler.

"Play" is perhaps a misleading term because *ta'ārof* in this regard is neither theatre nor a game. Iranians interacting with *ta'ārof* expressions and gestures are often demonstrating the reality of their situations. The politics of the situation is simply survival. The capriciousness of politics in Iran has been such that one has had to be able to play various roles along the ruler-

subject spectrum which *ta'ārof* reflects and for which it provides the means. In anticipation of unforeseen future twists of fate or turns of the wheel of fortune, one can at least verbally protect oneself by behaving always as if one's interaction partner(s) might someday wield the utmost power. At the same time, these social functions imply that certain aspects of *ta'ārof*, that is the particular expressions and gestures pertaining specifically to the interaction roles of ruler-subject relations, should fall into disuse if the nature of the political system in Iran and the attitudes of Iranians toward it were to change radically. Such a change, however, would have to be more significant than the dissolution of the monarchy in early 1979. After the departure of Mohammad Rezā Pahlavi, many Iranians began treating Ruhollāh Khomayni and his representatives in the same manner as they had treated the monarch and his representatives, with the special title *emām* serving as the equivalent for the royal politeness level expression *a'lāhazrat* ("you/he," used exclusively for the monarch).

Whether in a royal reception hall or underfoot at an audience Ruhollāh Khomayni might give, such carpets as the Kāshān *afshān* are material evidence of the same distinctive characteristics of Persian Iranian society which *ta'ārof* expressions represent.

QASHQĀ'I *BOTEH* MEDALLION CARPET

The Qashqā'is are a group of tribal peoples whose history from the sixteenth century has been associated with the south-central Iranian province of Fārs, specifically to the west and south of Shirāz. Their migrations still take them from south of Shirāz through Lor country up to the area near Ābādeh. The Qashqā'is, who speak Turkic dialects, are named after a Safavid leader to whom Shāh 'Abbās the Great gave authority over tribes south of Esfahān. Their power in Fārs province was considerable well into the twentieth century, with many roads there unsafe for travel without Qashqā'i permission. But as a nomadic people during the Pahlavi era, they fought a gradually losing battle in the face of Tehrān governmental centralization and a government policy restricting their migratory patterns. In spite of these sanctions, the Qashqā'is, heirs of both Central Asian Turkic people and ancient Iranian nomads, are as tenacious as any tribal group trying to maintain their traditional way of life in Iran today.

The weaving associated with the Qashqā'is is

in fact not exclusively the product of the Qashqā'i
tribes. Northwest of Shīrāz are located Lor tribal
groups, among them the Mamasānī, who weave
some carpets similar to Qashqā'i products. Then
to the east of Shīrāz is the Khamseh tribal confederation which weaves large quantities of carpets exhibiting designs shared with the Qashqā'is.
In the bazaars of Shīrāz and Tehrān, merchants
generally refer to the more coarsely woven carpets as Khamseh and the more finely woven as
Qashqā'i.[10]

Qashqā'i nomads and villagers produce a variety of carpet designs. One is a design featuring
one or more lion figures in the field. Referred
to as Fārs lion rugs, with lion figures that seem
more often the product of imagination than observation, these smaller rugs seem to have served
as special occasion pieces, to be laid out on the
tent floor when a guest was present, as if intend-
ing to equate the guest with the lion. (See Fig. 27.)
There are also simple, coarsely woven Qashqā'i
rugs called *gabeh* that feature merely jagged vertical lines or a single color field or simply arranged *boteh* shapes in the field. A third Qashqā'i
design consists of multiple medallions on the vertical axis or a central medallion with corner
medallions, each of which consists of a diamond,
lozenge, or hexagonal polygon and in it a scarab-
like figure that is often interpreted as a stylized
tarantula—as are some cruciform/stellate secondary motifs in some Torkaman *gol* carpets. Presumably, such tarantula shapes in tribal carpets
on tent floors would keep real tarantulas away
from the tent.

The quintessential Qashqā'i design is similar to
the scarab or tarantula medallion pattern. It features floral scatter throughout the field, which is
divided into two areas by a basically hexagonal
figure. But instead of scarab shapes bounded by
polygons, each of the five medallions consists of
eight *boteh* shapes. (See Fig. 34.)

The carpet exudes tribal qualities. The floral
scatter is intended to create an impression of
symmetry, but not many of the rosettes and
other floral shapes in one quarter of the field
appear in exactly the same place in the other
quarters. In addition, the carpet is all wool with
natural wool colors mixed in the warps; these
colors show as fringe at the top and bottom ends
of the carpet. The design is colorful, busy, and
not altogether regular. It has a certain spon-

Figure 33. Kāshān *afshān* design carpet.

taneity about it. The design seems surely to be
the Qashqā'i women's collective vision of perfect
springtime, the perfect garden, or the heavenly
paradise of the Koran.

The strongest evidence that Qashqā'i design
traditions are the transfer of observed nature in
its beautiful moments into the carpet fabric is the
pair of columns sometimes next to the lengthwise inner borders. These columns are the Qashqā'i weavers' representation of the columns still
standing on the great platform at the Achaemenid ruins at Persepolis, the monumental religious shrine begun by Darius in about 518 BCE.
Never finished, the site was further developed by
successive Achaemenid rulers and sacked and de-
stroyed by the forces of Alexander the Great in
330 BCE.[11]

At the end of each column, the weavers have
put a single mythological animal head. At Per-

---

10. Murray Eiland, "Introduction" to James Opie,
Tribal Rugs of Southern Persia, p. xi.

11. The handiest introduction to Persepolis is Jim
Hicks et al. *The Persians* (New York: Time-Life
Books, 1975).

sepolis, animal figures called "protoma" were originally set as two-headed figures atop the columns to support the beams and wooden roofs of various palaces and audience halls.

Even if Qashqā'i weavers were not aware of the historical significance of Persepolis, as they passed by the site on their migrations and developed the habit of including the columns in their carpets, they were recording nature as they saw it about them and continue to do so. The Persepolis columns are as much a part of their world as are the trees, flowers, shrubbery, and the like that become the floral scatter, stylized trees, and *boteh*s in their carpets. Interestingly, the original columns, which Qashqā'i weavers incorporate into the garden scenes of their carpets, were themselves conceived of by the planners and architects of Persepolis as groves of sacred trees. Consequently, they are part of the Qashqā'i carpet in two senses, even though the cosmopolitan, self-conscious imperial world of the Achaemenids was a wholly different Iranian world from that of contemporary Qashqā'is, whose struggle to per-

sist in their traditional nomadic ways seems certain to fail. Nearly 50 percent of the population of Iran was tribal in 1800. By 1980, less than 10 percent of the population was nomadic or seminomadic. Most Qashqā'i carpets produced today are made in villages. Some day the designation "Shirāz," as a label for where the carpets are marketed, may be more significant than the terms "Qashqā'i" or "Khamseh," the tribal groups to the west and east, respectively, of Shirāz, which originally produced them in nomadic settings. In fact, there is one version of the Qashqā'i *boteh* medallion that is already citified. Made in and around the city of Ābādeh, located on the main road between Shirāz and Esfahān, it features a bright red field, more regular placement of floral scatter, and white cotton warps. Mostly in smaller sizes, Ābādeh carpets, especially those that go through a chemical wash in Tehrān to mute their bright red before being retailed,[12] were popular among Westerners during the late 1960s and 1970s.

Interestingly, Qashqā'i carpets were not as popular with urban Iranians as with Westerners in the 1960s. The same might be said for Iranian tribal carpets, to which Westerners have seemed particularly attracted, as a whole. For many urban Iranians, caught up as they were in Pahlavi modernization, urbanization, and Westernization, tribal life and its art were, it would seem, alien. Yet Iranian tribal carpets became more popular within Iran in the 1970s for two reasons other than relative inexpensiveness. First seems to have been the realization, on the part of self-aware, urban Iranians worried about the viability of Iranian culture in the face of Westernization, that tribal carpets were a living part of their Iranian past. In particular, a carpet such as the Qashqā'i *boteh* medallion design, with its depiction of both traditional Persian garden and Persepolis elements, would provide a comforting backdrop to the lives of such concerned Iranians. As one Iranian art critic put it in 1971, "Persians have a reverence for the omnipresent past, we live in and with it. We cannot escape it; we even cling to it as a means of preserving our national identity. We have to prove to ourselves and to others where we belong and whence we are evolved. Perpetuating the ancient art forms has become a defense against the wholesale adoption of western social values."[13]

Figure 34. Qashqā'i *boteh* medallion with Persepolis columns carpet.

12. Opie, *Tribal Rugs of Southern Persia*, p. ix.
13. Emāmi, "Modern Persian Artists," p. 350.

Another motivation for the growing popularity of Persian tribal carpets among urban Iranians during the later Pahlavi years results from Westernization itself. Such Iranians were influenced by Western interest in such carpets and thereby became, as it were, "West-struck" (*gharbzadeh*) or imitative of Westerners in this regard as in other areas of Iranian life in the 1970s.[14] Thus, paradoxically, both the adoption of Western ways in urban Iranian life and the development of taste for a most traditional group of Persian carpets can be seen as indications of the great impact Westerners and their ideas were having on Iran during the pre-Khomayni era.

MASHHAD *LACHAK-TORANJ* WITH FLORAL FIELD CARPETS

If a single carpet design were used to illustrate the most popular image of Persian carpets outside of Iran, it would likely be the Kermān floral medallion with plain field design. (See Fig. 9.) If a single carpet design had to be chosen as the most popular Persian carpet design in the eyes of Iranians themselves, it might well be the design called *lachak-toranj*, which means "medallion and corner" elements. (See Fig. 35.) It refers to a traditional curvilinear floral design not unrelated to the Kermān in origin, but different from the most distinctive Kermāns in the floral shapes, leaves, and vines that reduce the role of the field color to a background color. The design appears in carpets from all over Iran, from Tabriz in the northwest to Mashhad in the east. More often than not, it is a medium-grade carpet with sturdy cotton warps and wefts and a relatively bright red as the field color. Iranian homemakers believe red shows dirt less than other colors and therefore use such carpets in living rooms and family rooms in which traffic and use are heavy. Although the design is readily available on the market in Europe and the United States, dealers tend to stock fewer pieces with the typical red field color which, together with the relatively high degree of floral activity in the field, makes such carpets somewhat out of place in many Western homes. In those

homes, the carpet must compete with a good deal of other furniture in room settings, whereas in Iran the carpet is the central and basic piece of furniture, sofas and chairs being arranged around and not on it.

The *lachak-toranj* design is obviously heir to Safavid curvilinear design traditions; it has no particular historical connection with Mashhad. The capital of the eastern province called Khorāsān, Mashhad lies on the Asian Highway, the road one takes to go overland from Europe to India, that is, the route from Istanbul through Ankara, Tabriz, Tehrān, Mashhad, Herāt, and Kābol.

As a growing metropolitan center in the 1960s and 1970s, Mashhad was the commercial hub of the whole province. In terms of carpets, this meant that village and tribal products of Baluch and Torkaman origin usually found their way to the Mashhad bazaar before being shipped to Tehrān. In addition, city carpet types from Birjand and Kāshmar and, of course, styles associated with Mashhad were also abundant. A major university, an important sugar beet factory, and relatively productive agriculture contributed to Mashhad's growth. But its most important feature, signified by its name which means "burial place of the martyr" in Persian, is the great shrine dedicated to Rezā, the eighth Shi'i Emām, who died there in 818 CE. Hundreds of thousands of pilgrims visit Mashhad annually to pay their respects to Emām Rezā. The pilgrimage and shrine have naturally assumed even greater importance since the establishment of the Islamic Republic of Iran in the spring of 1979.

The Mashhad *lachak-toranj* carpet type can be found in mosques all over Mashhad as well as in various rooms in the shrine precincts. It is, therefore, part of the symbolic religious traditions described earlier. But as an everyday sort of carpet in homes of all sorts in Iranian towns and cities, what it has to say about Iranian society may be a bit more mundane than what is implied by its religious associations.

First, there is a popular romantic interpretation of such designs. It is represented in a 1973 children's story by prominent short story writer Nāder Ebrāhimi (b. 1936) called "The Tale of the Carpet's Flowers."[15] The narrator begins

14. Prominent Iranian author and social critic Jalāl Āl-e Ahmad (1923–1969) denounced *gharbzadegi* [excessive fascination with or dependence upon Western ideas, methods, and goods] in a 1962 polemic of the same name that was circulated clandestinely in Iran during the later Pahlavi era. For more information on the subject, see *Iranian Society: An Anthology of Writings by Jalāl Āl-e Ahmad*, ed. Michael Hillmann (Lexington, Ky.: Mazda, 1982).

15. Nāder Ebrāhimi, *Qesseh-ye Golhā-ye Qāli* [The Tale of the Carpet's Flowers], drawings by Nuroddin Zarrin Kalak (Tehrān: Kānun-e Parvaresh-e Fekri-ye Kudakān va Nojavānān, 1973), 20 pp.

Figure 35. Mashhad *lachak-toranj* (corner element[s] and medallion) design carpet.

the story by asking his readers if they have ever
looked closely at the flowers in Persian carpets
or if they have ever realized that looking at floral
carpet designs is like sitting next to a vase full of
beautiful flowers or like having the sky with its
colorful stars brought down to earth or like sitting in a beautiful garden. He tells his readers:
"Look and see the world that exists on every
carpet, and what a beautiful world it is. . . .
On the carpet you do not see a single withered
flower . . ." He continues by saying that he wants
to relate a story about these floral carpet designs.

The story takes place once upon a time, perhaps
two thousand years ago or even much earlier. A
shepherd is living with his wife and two daughters in a very dry part of Iran in a year of drought.
He decides to take his flock to greener parts and
return when he hears that it has rained once again
in his home town. He leaves his family. A year
passes. The drought ends. The shepherd returns.
The family is happy again. His two daughters
ask him questions day and night about the green
places, the flowers, the seas, and the beauty of
nature he has seen. The shepherd cannot describe
all he has seen in words. So he decides to weave a
picture of it, with all the flowers, vines, leaves,
birds, everything beautiful he has seen.

He weaves the first floral Persian carpet. He
becomes very good at weaving such carpets,
which other people are willing to buy from him
at good prices. As time goes on, he changes the
designs, stylizes the flowers, tendrils, and leaves,
and uses all sorts of different colors in his carpets. Also, because his daughters are fascinated
by their father's weaving, they help him. Before
long, they take over the weaving. Because their
fingers are smaller and more slender, they produce more beautiful designs. The story ends with
the narrator observing that now, thousands of
years later, shepherds in Iran still tend their flocks
and their daughters still weave the most beautiful
carpets in the world with their small hands. The
text of the tale is accompanied by drawings of a
Kermān floral medallion with plain field carpet,
an Esfahān medallion with arabesque field carpet,
and a medallion and floral field carpet with a red
field color that might well be from Mashhad.

A second romantic interpretation of such carpets is that the girls who usually weave them
pour out their hearts in weaving, that the warps
and wefts of their carpets are their hopes and
dreams, and that the designs are their vision of
perfect beauty as a hoped-for future in the face
of a world that is not beautiful at all.

That these romantic interpretations have little
to do with the realities of carpet-weaving as employment and the weaver's function as a semi-
skilled laborer transferring the designer's vision
from cartoon to loom may be no more significant than the fact that many of the Iranians who
own such carpets want everything about them to
be positive, pleasant, and cheerful in their function as a setting of visual rest and repose in contrast to the harsh outside world.

Another side of the story has also been voiced,
one which refuses to ignore the kinds of lives
those who produce carpets must endure. A good
example is a story by Samad Behrangi (1939–1968),
Persian teacher in Āzarbāyjān, folklorist, writer
of children's stories, and social critic who died in
a never fully explained drowning incident in the
Aras River near the Iranian-Soviet border. Called
"The Little Sugar Beet Vendor," the story is told
by a village teacher whose school is visited one
day by a twelve-year-old boy who is obliged to
be the family breadwinner.[16] His smuggler father
was killed by the gendarmes. His mother is para-
lyzed. He now sells hot sugar beets in winter, although he and his older sister were formerly among
thirty or forty children employed in a village carpet workshop. The workshop was run by a *hāji*
from a nearby town who had set up the shop in
the village because labor was cheaper there than
in town. The sugar beet vendor's sister was making the equivalent of thirty American cents per
day, and he a little less. The workshop owner
made advances to the sister and even proposed
that she become his *sigheh* or legal temporary
wife. (The *hāji*'s wife and children were in town,
and he had already contracted for temporary
wives in four other villages.) The brother fought
the *hāji* to protect his sister, and they were both
fired. The sister eventually becomes engaged to
the son of the local breadmaker, and her brother
stays at home to help his invalid mother.

As the most popular design type in Iran, *lachak-
toranj* floral medallion and floral field carpets reflect both the traditional vision of Islamic paradise
and the connections between many curvilinear
carpet designs and traditional Iranian monarchy.
At the same time, the abundance of such carpets
indicates the importance of middle class life in

16. An English translation of "Pesarak-e Labu'for-
ush" [The Little Sugar Beet Vendor] is available in Samad Behrangi, *The Little Black Fish and Other Modern
Persian Stories*, trans. Mary and Eric Hooglund (Washington, D.C.: Three Continents, 1976), pp. 69–75.

Iranian cities. Owners of these carpets can afford to spend between $2,000 and $4,000 for a floor covering in an economy where the per capita annual income may not exceed $500. Such facts represent the other side of the story of Persian carpets. Their existence entails a workforce of mostly girls and women in villages, towns, and cities who weave to earn a mere subsistence living.

BALUCH TREE-OF-LIFE PRAYER CARPET

The distinctive Persian Baluch carpets are woven mostly by villagers in Khorāsān province in the region around Mashhad, especially to the south and east. Torbat-e Haydariyeh and Torbat-e Jām are two towns in the area associated with much Baluch weaving.

Persian Baluch designs owe their original inspiration to Torkaman traditions. The most common and popular Baluch carpets are characterized by distinctive reds and black with white as accent and trim, colored flat-weave webbing, small sizes, numerous borders and narrow fields, goat's hair selvage, and often, in contrast to much other Iranian tribal weaving, cotton warps. The field designs feature repeat and multiple medallion designs with Torkaman-inspired *gol*s as a primary field motif.

A very common and perhaps the most readily identifiable Persian Baluch carpet is a tree-of-life prayer carpet design. (See Fig. 36.) It is a design that offers eloquent testimony to significant as-

pects of Iranian village life in its complicated representation of pre-Islamic folk beliefs, the merging of such beliefs with Islamic values, and social and cultural dimensions of typical Iranian village environments.

The Baluch themselves are a distinct group of people long associated with Iran. Their homeland is called Baluchestān and Sistān, an area that includes the southeastern corner of Iran, that is from Bandar 'Abbās and Bam eastward, as well as the adjacent territory in Pakistan and southwestern parts of Afghanistan. It is as difficult a living environment as can be found in all of Iran. In their extremely dry, dusty, hot, and inhospitable territory, the Baluch nomads have never had a comfortable existence and have subsisted on the products of their sheep and goats. The extremely colorful Baluch-inspired carpets from the Zābol area seem a direct response of wishful thinking on the part of their weavers to vistas and lives that are harsh and barren.

But the bulk of the Baluch pile carpets woven in Iran are not woven in Baluchestān and Sistān, nor are they woven by Baluch nomads. Rather they are woven in villages and towns farther north in Khorāsān, where Baluch nomads were forced to migrate by Nāder Shāh Afshār, who ruled most of Iran from 1736 till his assassination in 1747. Modern Persian Baluch carpets are mostly woven by Baluch village girls and other village girls who have learned from the Baluch. The prayer carpet design featuring a stylized tree

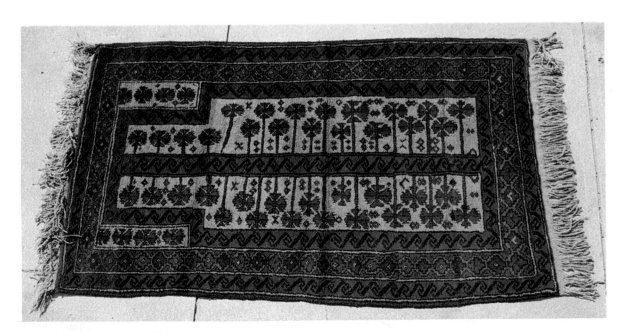

Figure 36. Baluch tree-of-life prayer carpet.

trunk, branches, and distinctive Baluch leaves in the field is one of the most common designs.

The depiction of a whole tree with trunk, branches, and leaves as the major field motif in tribal carpets of Lor, Baluch, and Zābol provenance, among others, seems at the very least an expression of hope or thankfulness for abundance or fertility, if not all the further meaning that "cosmic tree" or "tree of life" images can represent. However, there is a good case for assuming the relevance of this further meaning in the case of Baluch tree-of-life prayer carpets.

In Iran from ancient times plane trees (*Platanus vulgaris*) have been presumed holy. This holiness derives from the facts that plane trees are the largest on the Iranian plateau, that they are long-lived, and that they shade a large area. Also, because they shed their bark each year, some people believe that they thus rejuvenate themselves. There is also evidence to suggest that in ancient times it was believed that gods, fairies, and the souls of deceased tribal leaders either inhabited such trees or were manifested by them. Furthermore, in pre-Islamic Iran, these giant old plane trees had royal associations as well. Just as the king was presumed the human manifestation of divine blessings and powers, so the plane tree was their vegetal manifestation. These plane trees, as well as cypresses, date palms, and pomegranate trees, are still presumed holy in various areas of rural Iran.[17]

Another part of Iranian folk belief that may be of particular significance to the representation of trees in carpet designs is the notion that old plane trees bestow fertility and abundance on the earth and the family, help women to become pregnant and children to remain healthy, and cause commercial and other ventures to prosper.[18]

The Baluch people and those other village dwellers who have adopted Baluch weaving techniques and designs are, of course, devout Shi'i Moslems. Therefore, they naturally are heir to Islamicization of earlier Iranian notions and beliefs, among them the holiness of certain trees described in the Koran.

Then there are actual trees assumed to be sacred or blessed because a local saint or a relative of an *emām* is buried near them. For example, in the town of Torbat-e Jām, on the road from Mashhad to Herāt and named after the important fifteenth-century Sufi saint who is buried there, an old pistachio tree grows within the grave's enclosure. Throughout eastern Iran, there are many such trees to which local villagers and visitors, some of them pilgrims if there is an *emāmzādeh* or gravesite of a holy person nearby, tie pieces of cloth or bits of paper as oaths to perform certain deeds if their requests and wishes are granted.

Some of these traditional folk beliefs are surely related to popularity of the Baluch tree-of-life prayer carpet which is woven in hundreds of village communities from near the city of Zāhedān in the southeast corner of Iran all the way north to the town of Sarakhs on the Russian border north of Afghanistan. Part of the inspiration for such designs is also surely the great significance of trees with their greenness, coolness, and shade for the Baluch, whose homeland is particularly brown, barren, and harsh. The carpet, with its design of distinctive stick-like trunk and branches on which stylized serrated leaves are woven, may itself be a prayer for abundance, for what only Allāh can and presumably will give if people use the prayer rug for its specified purpose.

The Baluch tree-of-life prayer carpet speaks for a large segment of Iranian society who truly believe that fertility, abundant harvests, good weather, healthy children, and the like come directly from Allāh or through the intercession of his *emām*s and their relatives. They similarly believe that famine, infant mortality, childlessness, earthquakes, avalanches, springtime floods, and summer droughts are likewise fated, perhaps as Allāh's just punishment for sins or as his just tests of virtue. To tie an oath to a holy tree for them is a tried-and-true method of attempting to gain blessings and to reverse ill fortune. The abundance of Baluch tree-of-life prayer carpet designs, as well as of tree-of-life designs of Zābol, Lor, and Kurdish provenance, may be taken as evidence of the extent to which many rural people in Iran believe in the holiness of trees.

ARDABIL SHRINE DESIGN CARPETS

The specific design called the "Ardabil Shrine design" appears in carpets woven in Kāshān, Kermān, Yazd, Mashhad, Birjand, Tehrān, Tabrīz, and numerous other places in Iran where curvilinear designs are produced. There is probably not a single major dealer of Persian carpets in the West without at least one example of the design in stock. There are thousands, if not tens of thou-

---

17. Mehrdād Bahār, "Derakht-e Moqaddas" [The Holy Tree], *Alefbā* 1 (24 Shahrivar 1973): 93–96.

18. George Lechler, "The Tree of Life in Indo-European and Islamic Culture," *Ars Islamica* 4 (1937): 369–416.

Figure 37. Tabriz Ardabil Shrine design carpet.

sands, of examples in homes throughout England and the United States. More significant is the fact that it is a most popular design in Iran today and can be seen there as the living room or dining room carpet in thousands of homes.

Appreciation of the significance to Iranian society of the Ardabil Shrine design in modern carpets begins with a most important sixteenth-century Persian carpet prototype.

In 1843 an English traveler visited the famous Safiyoddin Shrine in the city of Ardabil. Shaykh Safiyoddin (d. 1334) was a Sufi leader and the eponymous founder of the Safavid dynasty (1501–1722). In his honor the Safavids built and maintained the shrine at Ardabil. The English traveler recorded the following observation about the shrine: "On the floor of the long lofty antechamber to the principal tombs were faded remains of what was once a very splendid carpet. At one extremity was woven the date of its make, some three hundred years ago."[19]

In order to repair Shaykh Safiyoddin's shrine, in which a prayer hall vault had collapsed, shrine authorities in the 1880s decided to finance the project through the sale of some shrine carpets. A Manchester importing firm active in Arāk and later an important carpet producer in Iran obtained the "faded remains," actually a pair of carpets of identical design but different size. Afterward a London carpet firm purchased the pair and offered them for sale for the amount of £2,500. The firm then undertook the repair of the better preserved of the pair by reweaving and replacing sections with material from the other. In 1893, after a successful fund-raising drive to raise what was then an extraordinary amount of money for an oriental carpet, the Victoria and Albert Museum acquired the repaired carpet, which was put on permanent display under glass and has subsequently been referred to as the "Ardabil carpet" or "Ardabil Shrine carpet."[20]

The importance of the Ardabil Shrine carpet as a beautiful carpet was immediately recognized, once it was put up for sale and displayed in 1892. The *London Times* called it "probably . . . the finest Persian carpet in the world . . ." The *Manchester Guardian* observed that "it is beyond doubt the finest carpet known to modern times . . . a magnificent carpet . . . which entirely beggars description." Since then, scarcely a book on oriental carpets has been published without at least lip service to the verdict of the press in 1892, and numerous illustrations of the carpet have been published.

---

19. Kurt Erdmann, *Seven Hundred Years of Oriental Carpets*, p. 30.

20. The Ardabil Shrine carpet on display at London's Victoria and Albert Museum is much illustrated. A color plate is available in Ian Bennett, ed., *Complete Illustrated Rugs and Carpets of the World*, p. 46. As for the remains of the other carpet in the original pair, whose middle section was intact, its existence was kept secret for a time. Later it was sold to an important American collector of oriental carpets "apparently on the condition that this fragment was never to be shown in England." In any case, the carpet remained unknown until the publication of the American collector's estate catalogue in 1910. At the auction of his collection the carpet was sold and later resold. It was later exhibited in Cleveland, St. Louis, Chicago, Detroit, and in 1931 at the exhibition of Persian art at Burlington House in London. Later, J. Paul Getty added the carpet to his collection. Finally, it was acquired permanently by the Los Angeles County Museum (Kurt Erdmann, *Seven Hundred Years of Oriental Carpets*, p. 32). Both the Victoria and Albert Museum and the Los Angeles County Museum have published brochures on the carpets.

The Ardabil Shrine carpet measures 11.5 × 5.34 meters for a total area of 61.5 square meters. Its warps and wefts are silk. Its pile features the Persian knot, approximately seventeen to nineteen knots per inch. Approximately thirty-two million knots constitute its pile. It may have taken several weavers in a royal workshop under the supervision of a master weaver about three years to complete. As for its design:

A yellow medallion filled with scrolling tendrils which end in arabesque leaves and which are interwoven with richly curved cloud bands occupies the centre of a dark-blue field. At the tips of this medallion sixteen ogees are arranged radially. Those on the main axes have a green ground. Of the three between these the central one has a red ground and the two flanking it are yellow. At both ends a large, red mosque lamp is suspended by four chains from the ogee on the main axis. A quarter of the same medallion with corresponding ogees appears in the corners of the field but without the mosque lamp. The ground is filled with floral scrolls of great complexity which finish at the edge of the field and do not contain the arabesque leaves and cloud bands of the medallion design. A clear distinction is made between the design of the field and the medallion. Strangely enough the border is not symmetrically constructed. The main stripe shows alternating red cartouches and green multifoils. The outer guard stripe has, on a red ground, a broadly designed reciprocally arranged design of palmette blossoms between pairs of arabesques, both in light blue. The inner guard stripe shows, on a yellow ground, a loosely drawn intermittent scrolling tendril and red cloud bands. A second red guard stripe with continuous tendrils is introduced next to the field. A rectangular cartouche with an inscription appears at that end of the carpet which was woven last.[21]

Modern carpets exhibiting the Ardabil Shrine design do not include the inscription, which contains two lines of poetry followed by the phrase "work of servant of the court Maqsud Kāshāni [in the year A.H.] 946." Since the inscription is at the upper end of the carpet field, the date presumably stands for the year in which it was finished: A.H. 946 = 1539/1540 CE. The significance of the signature has been much discussed in scholarly inquiry into where it might be assumed the carpet was woven. As for the two lines of poetry, they are the opening couplet in a *ghazal* poem of nine couplets by the most famous lyric poet in the thousand-year history of literature in the Persian language. This is Hāfez of Shirāz (ca. 1320–ca. 1390), the contemporary of Geoffrey Chaucer.

Hāfez's five hundred or so lyric compositions in the *ghazal* verse form have been appreciated by literate Iranians ever since as the culminating statements of a tradition of lyric verse that began five centuries earlier in the eastern Iranian area. As an apogee of Persian poetry, Hāfez's *ghazal*s are assumed to give voice to three separate themes. The first is the great tradition of secular love poetry in which the unworthy lover yearns for union with the unapproachable beloved, who is depicted as perfect beauty. The second is the distinctively Iranian Khayyāmic mood of the questioning individual who sees answers to life's problems and dilemmas neither in palace nor in piety, but rather in wholehearted dedication to the way of the heart, to the selfless giving of oneself in love. These two themes converge in a third, which is of special significance to the appreciation of potential symbolism in the Ardabil Shrine carpet. That is the gnostic stance that Hāfez assumes in his *ghazal*s in which what can be read as a lover's protestation of love for a perfect beloved is also interpreted as a Sufi's expression of commitment to love of the creator as the ultimate and perfect beloved whose perfection the lover glimpses in earthly beloveds made in the creator's image. Most Hāfez critics argue that Hāfez's verse is characterized by the presence of the rhetorical figure of *ihām* or "ambivalence," which is to say that both the mundane and spiritual worlds are assumed as concomitant levels of meaning in most of his *ghazal*s.

As for the *ghazal* in question, it reads as follows in its most popular variant:

1 Except for your threshold, there is no refuge in this world for me;
   except for this door, there is no shelter for my head.
2 When the enemy's sword is drawn, I throw down my shield in flight
   because I have no weapon except weeping and sighing.
3 Why should I turn away from the street where the tavern is,
   when I have no better way and path in this world than that?
4 If time and fate should consume my life's harvest in fire,
   tell them: set it afire, for my life does not have the value of a piece of straw for me.
5 I am the slave of the bewitching eye of that straight cypress-like one
   from the wine of whose pride not a glance is cast on anyone.
6 Do not search after torture and do whatever you will,
   for in our *shari'at* there is no sin but that.

---

21. Erdmann, *Seven Hundred Years of Oriental Carpets*, p. 29.

7 Go with reins drawn tight, o *shāh* of the land of
    beauty,
    for there are no paths where a lover of justice can be
    found.

8 As I see it from all of my affairs along the way
    there is no better refuge than the aid of his/her
    tresses.

9 Do not give over the treasury of Hāfez's heart to
    black tresses and a black beauty mark,
    for doing such things is not the work of any old
    black [slave].[22]

This Hāfezian *ghazal* describes a religion of
love with a *shari'at* or body of regulations and
laws, just as formal, orthodox Islam has its *shari'at*.
The worshiper in this religion is devoted to the
perfect beloved and to wine, either as consolation
for separation from the beloved or for the presumed inspiration resulting from its consump-
tion. Nothing is important except the beloved.
At this point the reader needs only to substitute
an image of God for images of an earthly beloved
to see that the *ghazal*'s statements work as well in
the Sufi's declaration of commitment to God as
in a lover's courtly love posture vis-à-vis a perfectly beautiful, aloof, and perhaps reproachful
beloved. In any case, this is how such *ghazals*
were read during the Safavid era (1501–1722). For
the Safavid court, such poetic allegory would
have been most familiar, since the Safavids themselves originated in the Ardabil area in the fourteenth century as a Sufi monastic order. They
became more political and militaristic as time
progressed, but never lost their sense of a special
religious mission. The first in the line to rule
over most of Iran was Esmā'il Shāh, who took
over leadership in 1499 and who associated him-
self with divinity. The most famous of the Safavid monarchs, Shāh 'Abbās the Great, who ruled
from 1587 to 1629, was responsible for the construction of the great shrine in Qom to Ma'sumeh
Fātemeh, the sister of Rezā, the eighth *emām* of
the Shi'is. Shāh 'Abbās also made a pilgrimage
on foot from Esfahān to Mashhad to visit the
shrine to Emām Rezā.

As for the presence of the first two lines of
Hāfez's *ghazal* in the inscription to the Ardabil Shrine carpet, one can only assume that the
sixteenth-century Safavid court that commis-

sioned and viewed the carpet saw the carpet in
the same terms as they interpreted Hāfez. This is
to say that the carpet design represented to them
a graphic depiction of qualities of God and spiritual reality drawn from garden imagery, just as
Hāfez's poem represented to them qualities of
God and man's proper attitude toward God
drawn from the imagery of human love vocabulary. Whether the Ardabil Shrine carpets were
actually woven with the shrine to Shaykh Safiyoddin in mind or not, that they ended up in
that shrine was wholly appropriate. Theirs was a
religious message, just as Shaykh Safiyoddin's life
was assumed to be and just as the architectural
decoration of the shrine itself is.

In fact, the pattern of the Ardabil Shrine carpets is a quintessential example of religious symbolism in Persian carpets. The corner quarter
medallions and floral field motifs disappear under
the borders surrounding the field, effecting in
the observer the sense that what is seen is merely
part of an infinite galaxy of such medallion
shapes and floral motifs. Concomitant with this
impression of infinity is a sense of equilibrium
between the central medallion and corner quarter
medallions, between the activity on the vertical

Figure 38. Kāshān Ardabil Shrine design carpet.

22. Hāfez, *Divān-e . . . Hāfez*, ed. Mohammad
Qazvini and Qāsem Ghani (Tehrān: Zavvār, 1941),
pp. 53–54, no. 76 (my translation). For more on
Hāfez, see Michael Hillmann, *Unity in the Ghazals
of Hāfez* (Minneapolis and Chicago: Bibliotheca Islamica, 1976).

axis consisting of central medallion with mosque lamps and the rest of the field consisting of the corner elements and floral motifs. The medallion itself exudes a sort of equilibrium in the balance between its sixteen protrusions and the sixteen ogival shapes beyond them. The observer cannot define a primary or enduring specific focus of attention. Thus, the infinity and indefinability of spiritual reality, that is, of Allāh, are here represented.

Aside from the mosque lamps that serve as pendants on the vertical axis and as obvious symbolic images of Allāh as the guiding light for humanity, the subject matter of the Ardabil Shrine design is obviously floral. The field seems a perfect garden; there are garden elements in the central medallion and corner quarter medallions as well. But the stylization of the floral elements, among them arabesques and *shāh 'abbāsi* motifs, intimates a denaturalization of nature. This persuades the observer that no earthly garden is intended, but rather the design is depicting the Islamic paradise. The intricacy of the design also effects a sense of dissolution of matter which reinforces the impression that a spiritual world is being depicted. There is nothing to keep the observer from supposing that he or she is looking from *terra firma* through the sky door with its cartouche and rosette and cloud band borders toward spiritual paradise.

Modern versions of the Ardabil Shrine design are a far cry from their Safavid prototypes in size, complexity of design, and colors. These differences are significant in sociological terms, but perhaps the most significant fact in this regard is that the original Ardabil Shrine carpets are in London and Los Angeles. In other words, Iranians today must make do with modern versions! This situation reflects Iran's position in general in the twentieth-century world: Iran is not even in control of its past and its history, much less of its future. To gain such control seems to be a basic instinctive motivation behind the Islamic Republic of Iran in its strident xenophobia and uncompromising religious nationalism.

As for the appearance of modern Ardabil Shrine design carpets in comparision with their sixteenth-century prototypes, the original color scheme is never replicated. For example, in popular room-size versions woven in Tabriz (see Fig. 37), typical contemporary Tabriz colors are used: darker reds, browns, greens, and other colors that can all be subsumed under the term earth tones, the same colors used in popular Tabriz

hunting and garden scene carpets, as well as medallion designs other than the Ardabil Shrine design. Kāshān versions sometimes exhibit the most typical Kāshān palette of blues, greys, and the like, or, along with versions from Yazd and elsewhere, the reds and other colors associated with popular everyday medallion carpets. (See Fig. 38.)

The monumental size of the original Ardabil Shrine carpets is rarely duplicated in modern versions, which are naturally intended for modern room-size spaces in Iranian living rooms and dining rooms. With the average modern version appearing in 6′ × 9′ to 9′ × 12′ dimensions as opposed to the 17′ × 34′ size of the carpet in the Victoria and Albert Museum, the contemporary Ardabil Shrine design carpet perforce exhibits less complexity of pattern and intricacy of detail. Typically decreased density of pile knots also contributes to the greater simplicity of design in modern versions. Secondary vine systems may be omitted, rounded figures may seem more angular, cloud bands may appear less serpentine, the space between the tips of the central medallion and the balancing ogival shapes may be much reduced. In many cases, the smaller the carpet is, the less appealing the attempt to replicate the Ardabil Shrine design on it becomes.

This is an aesthetic problem or issue with many modern versions of Safavid designs, which include almost all traditional curvilinear patterns that came into existence during that period, as well as hybrid designs such as familiar Hamadān, Heris, and Josheqān patterns. The fact of less complication and intricacy of motifs and patterns in modern Persian carpets is a main factor in their relative neglect in the carpet literature despite the proliferation of carpet books from the 1960s onward. In oriental carpet studies an antiquarian attitude prevails generally, along with a consensus that the "golden age" of Persian carpet production under the patronage of the Safavid dynasty (1501–1722) has never since been rivaled and that, except for glimmerings of greatness in some Qājār era (1796–1925) carpets, more recent products are pale, inferior, and imitative objects in comparison with their antecedents. It is a consensus that may seem both gratuitous and moot to any carpet *amateur* who lived and worked in Iran during the 1960s and 1970s and who may well have experienced on each successive visit to town and city bazaars, street shops, and Iranian homes the pleasant surprise of seeing carpets as appealing in their combination of utilitarian and decorative aspects as any carpets seen previously.

Such *amateurs* might conclude that contemporary Persian carpets—for example, various versions of the Ardabil Shrine design—in terms of size, materials, workmanship, and designs, seem generally to suit and reflect the needs, tastes, and life styles of people in Iran today. This conclusion may lead to the related questions as to how much more than this can be asked of a craft and how much more than this is needed to encourage a careful study of it.

A popular Iranian poet from the 1950s onward by the name of Nāder Nāderpur (b. 1929) reaches a similar conclusion in addressing the issue of differences between traditional and modernist Persian poetry in contemporary Iran. He says:

In our age in which electricity and the radio and the airplane have taken the place of the wind and quadrupeds and camel-litters and in which the whole world is interwoven, where is the opportunity for such prolixity and submissiveness in poetry . . . ? Our century is the century of storms and anxieties and haste, and the task of the poet in this century is the expeditious expression of a thousand sorts of feelings which surge in the souls of his or her contemporaries: the feeling of anguish and agitation during these tumultuous times of mere subsistence for millions of persons without a clear destiny, the feeling of anxiety from the misfortunes of war, from the leveling of homes in earthquakes, and the homelessness which is the lot of people in this age. No longer can there be all that entertainment and verbosity in poetry . . .[23]

---

23. Nāder Nāderpur, *Chashmhā va Dasthā* [Eyes and Hands] (Tehrān, 1954), p. 22 (my translation).

In terms of this analogy with Persian poetry, the Persian carpet *amateur* may recognize that traditional patterns have to be depicted on a much smaller surface with less intricacy of detail. In cultural terms, however, there is no implication of the superiority of the Safavid prototypes. They were the products of a small ruling elite and may thus have never been representative of Iranian life in general, whereas the less intricate modern versions woven in ordinary town and urban workshops and intended for the everyday Iranians who can afford to purchase them have much to say about the people who make and use them. These Iranians presumably feel comfortable with the implications of the traditional designs, as in the case of the Ardabil Shrine pattern. But rather than judge the reduced intricacy and complexity of modern Persian carpets as a sign of degeneration of a craft, one might look at the phenomenon in a twofold positive light. First, the intricate, complex, multilevel Safavid designs associated with the royal court have lost their elitist character through simplification as carpets have become a ubiquitous feature of general Iranian culture. Second, the greater simplicity in contemporary carpets may imply that the contemporary age has made demands on Iranians that preclude relaxed contemplation of complicated Safavid carpet designs.

Bibliography

More has been written about Persian carpets than about any other Iranian craft or art form. In English alone, hundreds of articles and books on oriental carpets, the bulk of them naturally devoted in part to Persian carpets, have been published in the last century. These include the scores of books translated into English from other European languages.

There are a number of bibliographies of publications on oriental carpets. But none of them is an annotated guide to the literature providing the *amateur*, academic researcher, merchant, or collector with references for locating reliable information on carpet types, technical aspects of weaving, or social and cultural dimensions. Nor is there a study of the available literature with suggestions as to how readers might judge the reliability of a book or article they come across.[1]

What follows is a guide and bibliography intended to meet the needs of Persian carpet *amateurs*, collectors, scholars, and merchants who may want more background information than this book provides and who need to examine on an ongoing basis as many illustrations of Persian carpets as possible. This guide and bibliography includes a partially annotated list of materials, mainly in English, mostly published from the mid-1950s onward. For earlier published materials there is the bibliography in Kurt Erdmann's *Oriental Carpets: An Essay on Their History* (1962). For continuing bibliographical information, *Hali: The International Journal of Oriental Carpets and Textiles* (1978–) and *The Oriental Rug Review* (1981–) are indispensable.

Erdmann's bibliography is divided into eight sections: (1) bibliographies, (2) works for general reference, (3) exhibitions, (4) museums, (5) private collections, (6) carpet auctions, (7) handbooks on more recent rugs, and (8) individual topics. In the chapter

on individual topics, there are sections on the origins of the rugs and the various groups of carpets. Four topics are covered in the origins section: fragments from Central Asia and related problems, early rug fragments (particularly from Egypt), rugs in miniatures and paintings, and Saljuq rugs. Ten topics are covered in the section on various groups of carpets: Cairene rugs (Mamluk and Ottoman), the Turkish rug, the Torkaman rug, the Persian rug collectively, "Polonaise" rugs, the flat-weave rugs of Kāshān, the "dragon rugs," the carpets of India, the Spanish rug, and the Chinese rug. Erdmann's bibliographical divisions are instructive; they are likewise illustrative of the breadth and complexity of the oriental carpet field. But for the study of modern Persian carpets, not all of his categories are necessary. Furthermore, in the appreciation of Persian carpets in the context of Iranian society, some materials perhaps not directly related to oriental carpets that Erdmann naturally did not cite seem to deserve attention. Examples include writing on Islamic art, Iranian society and culture, and aesthetics.

Kinds of Carpet Studies

The literature on Persian carpets itself has many forms. There are the handful of booklength studies devoted exclusively to Persian carpets. Then there are a great number of book-length introductory guides or handbooks of oriental rugs, in which Persian rugs generally receive detailed treatment. There are also numerous research articles on particular aspects of oriental rugs or particular themes generally on the subject of classical antique carpets. Guides to exhibitions and collection catalogues are two other important sorts of publications.

In evaluating the usefulness of the different sorts of publications dealing with Persian carpets, one might pay as much attention to the perspective of the author as to the nature of the publication. Six (sometimes distinct) perspectives are those of carpet *amateurs*, carpet merchants and entrepreneurs, collectors, carpet scholars or historians, Islamic art historians, and Iranologist area studies experts.

Michele Campana's *Oriental Carpets* (1969), an attractively printed and beautifully illustrated guide book first published in Italian, is representative of some recent introductory studies of oriental carpets by

---

1. Some oriental rug merchants seem aware of the public's need for guidance in utilizing the voluminous publications on the subject. See, for example, Jack Haldane-Izmidlian, "A Rug Book Overview," *Oriental Rug Review* 1, no. 4 (June 1981): 8–9, and 1, no. 11 (February 1982): 8–9; idem, "Rug Book Overview for the Beginner," *Oriental Rug Review* 2, no. 6 (September 1982): 13; and George O'Bannon, "A Beginner's Rug Book Survey," *Oriental Rug Review* 2, no. 6 (September 1982): 14.

carpet *amateurs* and merchants.[2] The author misspells the names of important carpet production centers, using "Feraghan" for Farāhān, "Naim" for Nā'in, "Heriz" for Heris, "Senneh" for Sanandaj, and "Ispahan" for Esfahān. He asserts that Kāshān, located between Tehrān and Esfahān, has a "tropical climate," that "the main population of Hamadān is Jewish," and that "in Khorāsān there are Arabs, Torkamans, Turks, Armenians, Jews, and a few Iranians." Campana terms the famous Ardabil Shrine carpet in the Victoria and Albert Museum "a hunting carpet" and asserts that "genuine knotting originated in Turkestan 2,000 years ago." In addition, the book exhibits numerous errors on various cultural subjects; for example: "for Orientals, rich and poor alike, carpets are almost the only furniture"; "carpets are laid on the doorstep to welcome all visitors"; and "orientals delight in continually inventing new designs and ideas." In fine, almost the only saving grace of Campana's book—by no means the most unreliable recent study—is a lengthy list of Italian painters who have depicted oriental carpets in their work.

Oriental carpet merchants are aware of and sensitive to criticism by art historians of "junk rug books" as "lacking useful information, . . . being badly written, and . . . plagiarizing each other's mistakes." Some merchants nevertheless argue that collectors want only books with color plates, pay little attention to the written text, and appreciate "lush color printing" above all.[3] The editors of the journal *Hali* have likewise observed that in the proliferation of carpet studies in recent years, the emphasis has been on picture guides in which "the text is strictly ephemeral."[4] Such a view, however, seems to beg the question. For even in a basically pictorial guide to oriental carpets, there would seem to be no reason for demonstrably false written material when accurate data are readily available. In the case of Persian carpets in particular, the simple fact is that most writers on the subject are not expert in the Persian language, Iranian culture or history, or other subjects where data necessary for the study of Persian carpets can be obtained.[5] On the other hand, if they were serious in their exclusive interest in illustrations

of carpets, they might eschew written commentary and produce books such as Jeffrey Weiss' pictorial survey called *Rugs* (1979).

Naturally the focus of the *amateur*-author is on his or her attraction to and personal impression of carpets, with the purpose of persuading others to appreciate carpets in the same way. On the other hand, the merchant-author focuses on those aspects of carpets of particular pertinence to potential customers. Charles W. Jacobsen, author of *Oriental Rugs: A Complete Guide* (1962)[6] and *Check Points on How to Buy Oriental Rugs* (1969), is a prominent example. The check points in Jacobsen's second book are certainly things the purchaser of a carpet ought to look for: irregularity or crookedness in shape, color changes across a swath, wrinkles, lack of flatness, edges curled under, unevenness of clipping, loose or bleeding colors, stains, holes, worn places, poorly constructed selvages, chemical washing, painting, saltwater or moth damage, double or *jofti* knots, use of dead wool, artificial antiquing, rewoven or sewn places, and determination of a fair price. On caring for carpets, Jacobsen has comments on sparse washing, vacuum cleaning, prevention of moth damage, professional cleaning, and spot removal.

As for *Oriental Rugs: A Complete Guide* (1962), it is divided into three sections entitled "General Discussion," "Description of Types in Alphabetical Order," and "Plates." Some of the plates depict carpets on the floor, an effective technique to remind readers that carpets as furniture have a context and rarely deserve to be treated as though they were paintings. In his general discussion, Jacobsen considers different classifications of carpets and, on the subject of Persian carpets, identifies "seven large weaving areas in Iran": (1) The Tabriz district, (2) the Hamadān district, (3) the Arāk district, (4) the Kermān district, (5) the Mashhad district, (6) the Shirāz district, and (7) the Bokhārā district.

Jacobsen's classification of carpet-weaving centers illustrates the limitations of such classification in oriental rug surveys. First, it sometimes becomes necessary to parallel designations that are basically not equivalent. For example, the "Mashhad district" designation refers to a geographical production and commercial center for a wide variety of city, village, and tribal carpets, whereas the "Bokhārā district" refers geographically to an area outside of Iran and, in terms of design, refers to Torkaman carpets exclusively. Instead of "Bokhārā," an appropriate district designation would identify the locale of Iranian production of Torkaman carpets, for example, the "Gorgān district" or the "Gonbad-e Qābus district." Second and more problematic in the classification of weaving centers is the possibility of omission of a center through oversight. There is no predetermined number of centers to serve as a checklist for the writer who wishes to cite "major"

2. Michele Campana, *Oriental Carpets*, trans. Adeline Hartcup (London: Paul Hamlyn, 1969).

3. A. S. Crosby, "The Critics Criticized," *Hali* 2 (1979): 230–231.

4. Editorial, *Hali* 2 (1979): 181.

5. See, for example, James Opie, "On the Road to Mazar—1973," *Oriental Rug Review* 2, no. 1 (April 1982): 1–2. Opie, the author of *Tribal Rugs of Southern Persia*, says that he knows very little Persian. In the words of Islamic art historian Walter B. Denny, "Rugs as Ideas," *Oriental Rug Review* 1, no. 12 (March 1982): 2, "The biggest problem with so much of the so-called 'rug scholarship' [is that] you have to hack your way through so much . . . drivel. For instance, few rug publications are refereed."

6. Charles W. Jacobsen, *Oriental Rugs: A Complete Guide* (Rutland, Vt.: Charles E. Tuttle, 1962).

centers. Jacobsen, for example, fails to cite Esfahān as a center, even though it is one of the most important in all of Iran. Nor does his classification identify Tehrān, Qom, Nā'in, and Kāshān as important centers of production. Third, when the merchant-author or collector-author attempts a comprehensive list of carpet types without having visited carpet production centers, numerous sorts of problems are likely to occur, as they do in Jacobsen's list of Persian rug types and in Ian Bennett's list in *Complete Illustrated Rugs and Carpets of the World* (1977). Examples include the description of such cities as Bijār and Malāyer as villages or the use of the term "Kurdish" for carpets implied as distinct from Bijār, Kermānshāh, and Sanandaj rugs, all of which are of Kurdish provenance.

The collector-turned-author often combines the *amateur*'s interest and the merchant's understanding of the market. However, unlike many merchants, carpet collectors generally show little interest in modern carpets. Also, unlike the *amateur* who is not a collector, the collector often has a special interest in a particular sort of carpet he or she has become interested in collecting. A good example is Joseph V. McMullan, whose personal collection is now a major part of the Metropolitan Museum of Art's premier North American collection. The various catalogues that have appeared in conjunction with exhibitions of carpets from his collection show a great interest in materials, colors, dimensions, and other minutiae, but no attempt is made at cultural or aesthetic appreciation.[7] His *Islamic Carpets* (1965) presents brilliant color plates including over twenty-five specimens of important Safavid and Qājār Persian carpet types.

In contrast, there is the carpet scholar or historian. Kurt Erdmann's *Oriental Carpets: An Essay on Their History* (1962) and *Seven Hundred Years of Oriental Carpets* (1970), Maurice S. Dimand's *Oriental Rugs in the Metropolitan Museum of Art* (1973), and the relevant chapters in Arthur Upham Pope's *A Survey of Persian Art* (1939, 1967) are generally accepted as valuable reference works. The two drawbacks for readers of these works who are interested in modern Persian carpets are antiquarian orientation and lack of concern with aesthetics or art criticism.

Another author type is the Islamic art historian, from whom, for various reasons, too little has been heard to date on the subject of Persian carpets.[8]

A final sort of author is the Iran area expert or Iranologist, who is interested in Persian carpets primarily because of their potential significance in the study of Iranian society and culture. This book is an example, albeit tentative and superficial, of an Iranian

studies perspective on Persian carpets. However, it is not necessarily the case that an area studies perspective will be more revealing or reliable than others in its scrutiny of Persian carpets. *The Simon and Schuster Book of Oriental Carpets* (1982) is an example of an extremely unreliable guide written by an "expert" in oriental languages affiliated with the Institute of Iranian Studies at the University of Venice.[9] Diagrams and drawings in the volume label obviously rectilinear elements as curvilinear and obviously vegetal or floral elements as geometric. The author refers to "The East" as a monolith. There is no documentation. There is much irrelevant material, even a full-page plate of a Sunday market in a Peruvian valley.

Evaluating Carpet Books

Even a reader coming to his or her first oriental carpet book can easily gauge the reliability of the book through a careful look at its index, bibliography, and preface.

If the preface implies that the subject of oriental carpets has never been treated before, that is an indication of one sort of vacuum in which the author is operating—a lack of familiarity with the considerable accumulated literature.

If the preface discusses "the Orient" or treats Asia as if it were homogeneous, another vacuum seems obvious, that is the lack of living experience in very different Asian societies that would persuade a writer to desist from thinking of or referring to Asia as a monolith.

If there are no notes referring to studies of Islam and Islamic art or to Iranian history and contemporary society, one can surmise that the text is likely to include a rehash of undocumented carpet lore or to emphasize the writer's personal, unsubstantiated impressions.

If no articles are cited in the bibliography and the only books there cited appear to be other introductory surveys, the reader can guess that the only knowledge reflected in the text is the personal, individual experience of the writer.

The index can be equally instructive in revealing the author's first-hand acquaintance with Persian carpets in their Iranian setting. Symptomatic of a lack of exposure to Iran are citations of such obsolete or inaccurate terms as "Bokhārā" for "Torkaman," "Lavar" or "Laver" for "Rāvar," "paisley" or "pear" for "*boteh*," "Senneh" for "Sanandaj," "Soltānābād" for "Arāk," "wine glass motif" for "flower calyx," "Yezd" for "Yazd," and reference to various cities as villages.

One can also check the accuracy of place names, geographical and historical data, and cultural information in reliable encyclopedias or other specialized studies.

---

7. According to Denny, "Rugs as Ideas," p. 4, McMullan was "a great collector and popularizer, not a scholar." As an art historian, Denny voices strong doubts about the seriousness and usefulness of oriental carpet literature authored by collectors and merchants.

8. Ibid.

9. Giovanni Curatola, *The Simon and Schuster Book of Oriental Carpets* (New York: Simon and Schuster, 1982). John J. Collins, Jr., *Oriental Rug Review* 2, no. 10 (January 1983): 10, terms it an example of "rug exploitation literature."

At the very least, any student of Persian carpets should be aware of and any serious comprehensive introduction to the subject should include Iranian place and tribal group names that identify major types of modern Persian carpets. A minimal checklist of fifty-five types appears at the end of Chapter 2.

In the following list of over seventy-five publications, only those studies of some specific use to students of modern Persian carpets are listed. From notes and other citations throughout the volume, the reader can guess by this point which are the most reliable studies. For example, no serious student of Persian carpets can afford not to have copies of Arthur Cecil Edwards, *The Persian Carpet*, and P. R. J. Ford, *The Oriental Carpet*. The several publications sponsored by the Iranian government are useful for their illustrations; e.g., Erwin Gans-Ruedin, *The Splendor of Persian Carpets*, and the two-volume catalogue by Simin Dāneshvar and Gertrude Nye Dorry, *Masterpieces of Persian Carpet* and *Persian Carpet Appreciation*. Annotations after bibliography items advise the reader as to the specific usefulness of other studies. If an annotation merely cites the illustrations, the reader can assume that the text is not reliable.

Few articles are listed separately. Such journals as *Hali* and *Oriental Rug Review* need to be perused regularly. Relevant articles from them, the now defunct *Honar va Mardom, Apollo, Oriental Art*, and the like are cited in notes.

Many more or less popular or readily available books, including those by Caroline Bosley (1980), Robert de Calatchi (1967), Luciano Coen and Louise Duncan (1978), Jack Frances (1970), Arthur T. Gregorian (1967), Herman Haack (1960), Nathaniel Harris (1977), Albrecht Hopf (1962, 1967), George Izmidlian (1977), Charles W. Jacobsen (1962), Stefan Milhofer (1976), Ignace Schlosser (1963), Kudret H. Turkhan (1969), and Moddie Jeffries Williams (1967), among others, have not been cited because their plates and commentary seemed to add little to materials available in more reliable or better-illustrated studies. Older studies, which of course provide no information about Persian carpets since World War II, are likewise not cited except in the case of important scholarly works. Also unlisted are important studies on specific non-Iranian oriental carpets by Hans Bidder (1964), Philip Denwood (1974), Murray Eiland (1979), Kurt Erdmann (1977), John Haskins (1973), Johann Iten-Maritz (1977), Lyatif Kerimov (1961), H. A. Lorentz (1973), Ulrich Schürmann (1974), Jeanne Weeks and Donald Treganowan (1969), and Şerare Yetkin (1978). Some of these studies, however, as well as other important works on textiles, Islamic art, and other topics, are cited in the text if and when they have been consulted or used as sources.

Annotated List of Publications

Aschenbrenner, Eric. *Oriental Rugs, Volume 2: Persian*. Munich: Oriental Textile Museum, 1981. 264 pp.

Azadi, Siawosch. *Persian Carpets*. Translated by Robert Pinner. Tehran: Carpet Museum, 1977. 115 pp.
———. *Turkoman Carpets and the Ethnographic Significance of Their Ornaments*. Translated by Robert Pinner. Fishguard, Wales: Crosby Press, 1975. 47 [+39] pp. Includes a color-coded map of Torkaman tribal group areas and a comprehensive bibliography. Fifty-five color plates of mostly nineteenth-century pieces from tent bands to main carpets.
Beattie, May H. *Carpets of Central Persia, with Special Reference to Rugs of Kirman*. London: World of Islam Festival, 1976. 104 pp.
———. "On the Making of Carpets." In *Islamic Carpets from the Joseph V. McMullan Collection*, pp. 22–29. London: Arts Council of Great Britain, 1972.
Beh'āzin, M. E. *Ketāb-e Qāli-ye Irān* [The Book of the Carpet of Iran]. Tehrān: Ebn-e Sinā, 1965/1966. 153 pp.
Bennett, Ian. *Book of Oriental Carpets and Rugs*. New York: Hamlyn, 1972. 128 pp.
Color plates of classical antique Esfahān, Farāhān, Hamadān, Herāt, Heris, Josheqān, Kāshān, Kermān, Kurdish, Polonaise, and Shirāz carpets, as well as of some of the world's most famous Persian carpets: the Pazyryk carpet, the Ardabil Shrine carpet, the Chelsea carpet, the Milan hunting carpet, the Milan animal and floral with medallion and inscription carpet, the Vienna silk hunting carpet, the Vienna animal and floral carpet, the Paris (half of) animal and tree with medallion carpet, and the Victoria and Albert rose ground vase carpet.
———, ed. *Complete Illustrated Rugs and Carpets of the World*. New York: A & W Publishers, 1977. 352 pp. Includes plates of European paintings featuring oriental rugs and of the following sorts of nineteenth- and twentieth-century Persian carpets: Bakhtiyāri, Baluch, Esfahān, Farāhān, Heris, Josheqān, Kermān, Kurdish, Qashqā'i, and Torkaman.
Biggs, Robert, ed. *Discoveries from Kurdish Looms*. Chicago: Northwestern University, 1983. 116 pp. An exhibition catalogue featuring useful short essays on the Iranian Kurds and their weaving traditions, and over forty illustrations of mostly pre–World War II Iranian Kurdish *gelim*, flatweave, and pile weavings.
Black, David, and Clive Loveless, with essays by Jon Thompson and others. *Rugs of the Wandering Baluchi*. London: David Black Oriental Carpets, 1976. 32 pp. [+ 45 unnumbered pp.]
———, eds. *Woven Gardens: Nomad and Village Rugs of the Fars Province of Southern Persia*. London: David Black Oriental Carpets, 1979. 149 pp.
Bode, Wilhelm von, revised by Ernst Kühnel. *Antique Rugs from the Near East*. 4th rev. ed. Translated by C. G. Ellis. London: Bell, 1970 (translation first published in 1958). 184 pp. A study of classical antique Islamic carpets with chapters on the carpets of Turkey, rugs of the Caucasus, Egyptian carpets, the carpets of Persia,

and Mughal rugs from India. Persian carpets discussed and illustrated are early Persian rugs (earliest discoveries, rugs in miniature paintings); medallion carpets (carpets with floral decor, animal carpets, so-called Portuguese carpets), vine scroll patterns (arabesque rugs, so-called Herat rugs), compartment designs, rugs with progressive designs (so-called vase carpets, shrub and tree rugs, garden rugs), pictorial rugs, so-called Polonaise rugs, and prayer rugs.

Boston Museum Journal 69, nos. 355–356 (1971).

On the sixteenth-century Boston hunting carpet.

Cammann, Schuyler V. R. "Cosmic Symbolism on Carpets from the Sanguszko Group." In *Studies in Art and Literature of the Near East in Honor of Richard Ettinghausen*, edited by Peter Chelkowski, pp. 181–208. New York: New York University, 1974.

———. "'Paradox' in Persian Carpet Patterns." *Hali* 1 (1978): 250–257.

———. "Symbolic Meanings in Oriental Rug Patterns: I, II, III." *Textile Museum Journal* 3, no. 3 (December 1972): 5–54.

———. "The Systematic Study of Oriental Rugs: Techniques and Patterns." *Journal of the American Oriental Society* 95 (1975): 248–260.

Review of May H. Beattie, *The Thyssen-Bornemisza Collection of Oriental Rugs* (1972).

Dāneshvar, Simin, and Gertrude Nye Dorry. *Masterpieces of Persian Carpet*. Tehran: Iran Carpet Company; Pishgar Publishing & Advertising Company, 1973.

One hundred color plates accompanied by not wholly accurate descriptions in English and Persian of modern Persian carpets of Ābādeh, Arāk, Ardabil, Birjand, Esfahān, Gonābād, Hamadān, Kāshān, Kermān, Kurdish, Mahallāt, Malāyer, Mashhad, Nā'in, Qazvin, Qom, Rafsanjān, Semnān, Shāhrezā, Tabriz, Tehrān, Torkaman, and Zābol provenance.

———. *Persian Carpet Appreciation*. Tehran: Iran Carpet Company, 1974.

A continuation of *Masterpieces of Persian Carpet*. One hundred color plates and accompanying descriptions in English and Persian of Persian carpets of Ābādeh, Arāk, Ardabil, Ardestān, Bakhtiyāri, Birjand, Esfahān, Hamadān, Kāshān, Kāshmar, Kermān, Khorāsān, Kurdish, Meshkinshahr, Nā'in, Qom, Rafsanjān, Semnān, Shāhrezā, Tabriz, Tehrān, Yalameh, and Yazd provenance. Introductory essay identifies and describes nineteen main patterns and subpatterns in Persian carpets.

Dhamija, Jasleen. *Living Tradition of Iran's Crafts*. New Delhi: Vikas, 1979. x, 81 [+8] pp.

Dimand, Maurice S., with one chapter by Jean Mailey. *Oriental Rugs in the Metropolitan Museum of Art*. Greenwich, Conn.: New York Graphic Society, 1973. ix, 353 pp.

One chapter on "Rugs of Persia": Mongol period

(fourteenth century), Timurid period (fifteenth century), Turkoman rugs of Northwest Persia (end of fifteenth century), Safavid period (sixteenth to early eighteenth century), and nineteenth and twentieth centuries. No discussion of modern Persian carpets. Important and detailed discussion of Safavid types.

Edwards, Arthur Cecil. *The Persian Carpet: A Survey of the Carpet Weaving Industry of Persia*. Rev. ed. London: Duckworth, 1975. (1st ed., 1953.) xvi, 384 pp.

An important study of the industry up to 1952 that discusses carpets in the following areas: Tabriz (including Heris, Ardabil, and Meshkinshahr); Hamadān; Torkaman rugs; Mashhad (including Birjand); Baluch rugs; Kermān (including Afshār); tribal and village rugs of Fārs (e.g., Ābādeh, Khamseh, Qashqā'i); Esfahān (including Bakhtiyāri, Josheqān, and Nā'in); and Kāshān and Qom. Numerous, mostly black-and-white plates of the major Persian carpet types.

Eiland, Murray L. *Oriental Rugs: A New Comprehensive Guide*. Rev. ed. Boston: Little, Brown and Company, 1981. (Revised and expanded version of the 1976 edition.) 294 pp.

Makes at least minimal use of available research and attempts to go beyond a rehashing of the lore. Eight chapters: history and development, the elements of design, the problem of dyes, the construction of carpets, the rugs of Persia, Turkish rugs, Turkoman rugs, and rugs of the Caucasus. Numerous black-and-white photographs and some color plates of mostly nineteenth-century examples of the following sorts of Persian carpets: Afshār, Arāk, Baluch, Hamadān, Kāshān, Mashhad, Qashqā'i/Khamseh, Tabriz, and Torkaman.

Encyclopaedia Britannica, 15th ed. (1974) s.v. "Rugs and Carpets."

Erdmann, Kurt. *Oriental Carpets: An Essay on Their History*. Translated by C. G. Ellis. New York: Universe, 1962. (Translation first published in 1960.) 80 pp.

———. *Seven Hundred Years of Oriental Carpets*. Edited by Hanna Erdmann. Translated by May H. Beattie and Hildegard Herzog. Berkeley: University of California Press, 1970. iii, 238 pp.

Important essays on various topics relating to oriental rug history and classical antique carpet types.

Ettinghausen, Richard, et al. *Prayer Rugs*. Washington, D.C.: Textile Museum, 1974. 139 pp.

Features: Richard Ettinghausen, "The Early History, Use and Iconography of the Prayer Rug," pp. 10–25.

Fokker, Nicolas. *Oriental Carpets for Today*. Translated by Keith Bradfield. Garden City, N.Y.: Doubleday, 1973. 135 pp.

Color plates of Persian carpets of Ābādeh, Afshār, Arāk, Ardabil, Bakhtiyāri, Baluch, Esfahān, Farā-

hān, Hamadān, Heris, Kalārdasht, Karājeh, Kāshān, Kermān, Kurdish, Malāyer, Mashhad, Mazlaqān, Nā'in, Qashqā'i/Khamseh, Qom, Sarāb,
Semnān, Shāhsavan, Tabriz, Tafresh, Torkaman, Tuyserkān, Varāmin, Yazd, and Zanjān
provenance.

Ford, P. R. J. *The Oriental Carpet: A History and
Guide to Traditional Motifs, Patterns, and Symbols.*
New York: Abrams, 1981. 352 pp.

The best available "hand book on rug identification . . . to help the buyer narrow his choice and
gauge value for money by recognizing styles and
places of origin." Includes illustrations and descriptions of nearly six hundred rug types available on the market today, including the following
Persian carpets: Ābādeh, Afshār, Ahar, Arāk, Ardabil, Bakhtiyāri, Baluch, Behbahān, Bijār, Birjand, Borujerd, Esfahān, Fārs lion, Hamadān,
Heris, Josheqān, Kalārdasht, Karājeh, Kāshān,
Kermān, Khamseh, Khorāsān, Khorramābād,
Lor, Malāyer, Mashhad, Maymeh, Meshkinshahr,
Nahāvand, Nā'in, Qashqā'i, Qom, Quchān, Sanandaj, Sarāb, Shahr-e Kord, Shāhsavan, Shirāz,
Tabriz, Tafresh, Torkaman, Tuyserkān, Varāmin,
Yalameh, Yazd, and Zanjān. These and other non-
Persian carpet illustrations and descriptions are
commonsensically grouped in helpful categories
of "universal" (e.g., *boteh, herāti,* prayer), "geo-
metric," and "floral" designs.

Formenton, Fabio. *Oriental Rugs and Carpets.* Translated by Pauline L. Phillips. New York: McGraw-
Hill, 1972. 251 [+ 1] pp.

Color plates of carpets of Ābādeh, Afshār, Arāk,
Ardabil, Bakhtiyāri, Baluch, Birjand, Borujerd,
Esfahān, Farāhān, Hamadān, Heris, Josheqān,
Kāshān, Kermān, Khorāsān, Kurdish, Lor, Mal-
āyer, Mazlaqān, Nā'in, Qashqā'i/Khamseh, Qom,
Rāvar, Tabriz, Tehrān, Torkaman, and Varāmin
provenance.

Gans-Ruedin, Erwin. *Antique Oriental Rugs.* Translated by Richard and Elizabeth Bartlett. New York:
Kodansha, 1975. 481 pp.

Black-and-white and color plates of nineteenth- and
early twentieth-century specimens of the following
sorts of Persian carpets: Arāk, Baluch, Borujerd,
Esfahān, Farāhān, Hamadān, Heris, Josheqān,
Kāshān, Kermān, Kurdish, Malāyer, Mashhad,
Meshkinshahr, Nayriz, Qashqā'i/Khamseh, Tabriz, Tehrān, Torkaman, and Varāmin.

———. *The Connoisseur's Guide to Oriental Carpets.*
Translated by Valerie Howard. Rutland, Vt.: C. E.
Tuttle, 1971. 431 pp.

Nearly one hundred black-and-white and color
plates accompanied by drawings and descriptive
blurbs of carpets of Ābādeh, Afshār, Ahar,
Ahmadābād, Arāk, Ardabil, Asadābād, Bahārlu,
Bakhshāyesh, Bakhtiyāri, Baluch, Bolvardi, Borujerd, Hamadān, Heris, Josheqān, Kalārdasht, Karājeh, Kāshān, Kermān, Kolvanaq, Kurdish,

Malāyer, Mashhad, Mehrebān, Meshkinshahr,
Nā'in, Nayriz, Qashqā'i/Khamseh, Qom, Sarāb,
Sonqor, Tabriz, Tuyserkān, Varāmin, Yalameh,
and Zanjān provenance. In sections devoted to
Central Asia and Afghanistan, typical Torkaman
and Afghān carpets are illustrated.

———. *The Great Book of Oriental Carpets.* Translated
by Valerie Howard. New York: Harper and Row,
1983. 180 pp.

Thirty-nine excellent color plates of nineteenth-
and twentieth-century examples of carpets of
Afshār, Arāk, Ardabil, Bakhtiyāri, Baluch, Bijār,
Birjand, Esfahān, Farāhān, Hamadān, Heris,
Josheqān, Kalārdasht, Karājeh, Kāshān, Kermān,
Koliāyeh, Lorestān, Mahāl, Mashhad, Mazlaqān,
Meshkinshahr, Nā'in, Qashqā'i, Qom, Sanandaj,
Sarāb, Semnān, Shirāz, Tabriz, Tafresh,
Torkaman, Varāmin, Yalameh, and Yazd prove-
nance. Nearly all of the plates and commentaries
are reprinted (without acknowledgment) from
earlier volumes by Gans-Ruedin.

———. *The Splendor of Persian Carpets.* Translated by
Valerie Howard with Jacqueline Bazin. New York:
Rizzoli, 1978. 546 [+20] pp.

Color plates of the Pazyryk carpet and important
pre-1800 Persian carpets and of nineteenth- and
twentieth-century Persian carpets of Ābādeh,
Afshār, Arāk, Bakhshāyesh, Bakhtiyāri, Baluch,
Birjand, Borujerd, Esfahān, Farāhān, Hamadān,
Heris, Josheqān, Kāshān, Kermān, Khorāsān,
Kurdish, Lor, Malāyer, Mashhad, Mazlaqān,
Meshkinshahr, Nā'in, Qashqā'i/Khamseh, Qoltaq,
Qom, Sarāb, Semnān, Tabriz, Tafresh, Tehrān,
Torkaman, Varāmin, Yalameh, and Yazd prove-
nance. Among important sixteenth-century Safa-
vid carpets illustrated: Vienna garden carpet,
Milan hunting carpet, Chelsea carpet, Ardabil
Shrine carpet, Anhalt medallion and arabesque
carpet, Paris (half of) animal and tree with medal-
lion carpet, Vienna multiple medallion carpet,
National Gallery medallion and animal carpet,
Milan animal and floral with medallion and inscription carpet, Metropolitan Northwest Persia
prayer carpet, Vienna animal and floral carpet,
Boston hunting carpet, and Milan floral carpet
with arabesques.

Gluck, Jay, and Sumi Hiramoto Gluck, eds. *A Survey of
Persian Handicraft: A Pictorial Introduction to the Con-
temporary Folk Arts and Art Crafts of Modern Iran.*
New York: Bank Melli Iran, 1977. 416 pp.

Golombek, L. V. "Anatomy of a Mosque." In *Iranian
Civilization and Culture,* edited by Charles J. Adams,
pp. 5–14. Montreal: McGill University, Institute of
Islamic Studies, 1972.

*Hali: The International Journal of Oriental Carpets and
Textiles,* 1978–.

"The first journal dedicated to covering all aspects
of the Oriental carpet and textile world," *Hali* is
invaluable for the collector as a guide to the best

oriental carpets on the market today. For the scholar, *Hali* offers brief technical articles and reviews of recent publications in both German and English.

Haydari, 'Ali Rezā. "Qāli'bāfi dar Irān" [Carpetweaving in Iran]. *Sokhan* 10 (1959/1960): 350–355, 456–460, 581–587, 693–696, 808–812, 916–918, 1027–1033.

Herbert, Janice Summers. *Oriental Rugs: The Illustrated Guide—A Handbook for the American Buyer*. Rev. and expan. ed. New York: Macmillan, 1982. 175 pp.

   Color plates of carpets of Ābādeh, Afshār, Arāk, Ardabil, Baluch, Birjand, Esfahān, Farāhān, Hamadān, Heris, Josheqān, Karājeh, Kāshān, Kermān, Khorāsān, Kurdish, Malāyer, Mashhad, Meshkinshahr, Nā'in, Qashqā'i/Khamseh, Qom, Tabriz, Torkaman, and Yalameh provenance.

Honar va Mardom [Art and People].

   Important Pahlavi-era monthly published by the Iranian Ministry of Culture and Arts, featuring numerous articles on Persian carpet motifs and patterns.

Housego, Jenny. *Tribal Rugs: An Introduction to the Weaving of the Tribes of Iran*. New York: Van Nostrand Reinhold, 1978. 174 pp.

   Includes a map of the main tribal areas of Iran and illustrations of the Afshār, Bakhtiyāri, Khamseh, Kurdish, Qashqā'i, and Shāhsavan peoples.

Hübel, Reinhard G. *The Book of Carpets*. Translated by Katherine Watson. New York: Praeger, 1970. 348 pp.

   Early history and the spread of the knotted carpet; production, structure, and material; colors and dyeing; design and pattern; names and terms for carpets; Turkish carpets; Caucasian carpets; Persian (Iranian) carpets; Torkaman carpets; the carpets of East Turkestan; Chinese carpets; carpets from other countries; age and authenticity; purchase, laying, care; on collecting oriental carpets. Numerous black-and-white photographs and the following color plates of Persian carpet types: Baluch, Farāhān, Kermān, Meshkinshahr, Qashqā'i, and Torkaman.

Jacobsen, Charles W. *Check Points on How to Buy Oriental Rugs*. Rutland, Vt., and Tokyo: Charles E. Tuttle, 1969. 208 pp.

Jerrehian, Aram, Jr. *Oriental Rug Primer: Buying and Understanding New Oriental Rugs*. Philadelphia: Running Press, 1980. 223 pp.

   A paperback aiming to provide an inexpensive introduction to the subject. Mediocre color plates of carpets of Ābādeh, Afshār, Arāk, Ardabil, Bakhtiyāri, Baluch, Esfahān, Hamadān, Heris, Josheqān, Karājeh, Kāshān, Kermān, Kurdish, Meshkinshahr, Nā'in, Qom, Sarāb, Shirāz, Tabriz, Torkaman, and Yalameh provenance.

Keshishian, Mark. *Guide to Oriental Rugs*. New York: Keller, 1970. xvii, 134 pp.

   Information on oriental carpet weaving in Corfu

and Athens in the 1920s and color plates of Ābādeh, Ahar, Arāk, Baluch, Esfahān, Hamadān, Heris, Josheqān, Karājeh, Kāshān, Kermān, Kurdish, Mashhad, Nā'in, Qashqā'i, Qom, Tabriz, Tehrān, and Torkaman carpets.

Khānmohammad Āzari, Bahman. "Qāli-ye Irān-rā Beshenasim, Qāli-ye Kermān, Gowhar-e Jāvdāneh-ye Irān" [Let's Get Acquainted with the Iranian Carpet, the Kermān Carpet, Iran's Immortal Jewel]. *Honar va Mardom*, no. 174 (Farvardin 1977): 18–25; no. 175 (Ordibehesht 1977): 25–33.

Konieczny, M. G. *Textiles of Baluchistan*. London: British Museum, 1979. 77 pp.

Kühnel, Ernst. *The Arabesque: Meaning and Transformation of an Ornament*. Translated by Richard Ettinghausen. Graz, Austria: Verlag für Sammler, 1977. 80 pp.

Landreau, Anthony N., ed. *Yörük: The Nomadic Weaving Tradition of the Middle East*. Pittsburgh: Museum of Art, Carnegie Institute, 1978. 144 pp.

   Exhibition catalogue. Includes: John T. Wertime, "The Names, Types and Functions of Nomadic Weaving in Iran" (pp. 23–26); Jenney Housego and Raoul Tschebull, "Northwestern Iran and Caucasus" (pp. 42–48); John T. Wertime, "The Lors and Bakhtiyaris" (pp. 49–52); Joan Allgrove, "The Qashqā'i" (pp. 52–55); Walter B. Denny, "Türkmen Rugs in Historical Perspective" (pp. 55–59); and George W. O'Bannon, "Baluchi Rugs" (pp. 62–64).

Lanier, Mildred B. *English and Oriental Carpets at Williamsburg*. Williamsburg, Va.: Colonial Williamsburg Foundation, 1975. xiii, 132 pp.

   Color plates of thirty-five classical antique Persian, Turkish, and Caucasus carpets.

Lion Rugs from Fārs. Oshkosh, Wisc.: Castle-Pierce, 1974. 62 pp.

   An exhibition guide with forty-one plates together with descriptions of Qashqā'i, Khamseh, Bakhtiyāri, and Lor carpets featuring one or more lion figures as major motifs in the field pattern. Features a foreword by Richard Ettinghausen.

Loges, Werner. *Turkoman Tribal Rugs*. Translated by Raoul Tschebull. Atlantic Highlands, N.J.: Humanities Press, 1980. 204 pp.

   One hundred seventeen color plates of mostly nineteenth-century Torkaman pile carpet articles, including Tekkeh, Salor, Saryk, Yomut, Chodor, Kizilayak, Ersāri, and Arabatshi carpets.

Macey, R. E. G. *Oriental Prayer Rugs*. Leigh-on-Sea: F. Lewis, 1961. 24 pp.

   Sixty-five black-and-white plates of prayer rugs from Turkey, the Caucasus, Iran, and Central Asia. Ignores such prayer rug types as various Torkaman and Baluch *jānamāzis*.

McMullan, Joseph V. *Islamic Carpets*. New York: Near Eastern Art Research Center, 1965. 385 pp.

   A catalogue of 152 mostly nomad and village rugs of the eighteenth and nineteenth centuries, all of them illustrated, 122 in brilliant color plates. Divided into sections on Mamluk, Turkish court manufactory, and Mughal rugs; Persian rugs: School of Shāh Tahmāsp; Persian rugs: School of Shāh 'Abbās; South Persian rugs; Persian rugs: nineteenth century; Classical Turkish rugs; "Transylvanian" rugs; Turkish village rugs: eighteenth and nineteenth centuries; Torkaman rugs; and Mongol saddle rugs.

Makki'zādeh, Mahmud, and Nāser Āqājani. *Qāli-ye Irān* [The Iranian Carpet]. Yazd: Enteshārāt-e 'Asr, n.d. 24 pp.

Neff, Ivan C., and Carol V. Maggs. *Dictionary of Oriental Rugs*. New York: Van Nostrand Reinhold, 1979. 238 pp.

An inaccurate compilation attempting to provide a dictionary guide to nomenclature and place names. Includes a color relief map of "Major Oriental Rug-Weaving Areas" and color plates of the following sorts of Persian carpets: Arāk, Baluch, Esfahān, Farāhān, Hamadān, Heris, Kāshān, Kermān, Khorāsān, Kurdish, Nā'in, Nayriz, Qashqā'i, Qom, Tabriz, Torkaman, and Varāmin. Discussion of carpet identification by weave with plates of details of carpet backsides.

O'Bannon, George W. *The Turkoman Carpet*. London: Duckworth, 1974. 168 pp.

Concentrates on the Torkaman carpets from Afghanistan, which the author opines "are of the best quality of all Torkaman carpets being produced today." Three pages on Iranian Torkaman carpets.

Opie, James. *Tribal Rugs of Southern Persia*. Portland, Ore.: James Opie Oriental Rugs, 1981. xi, 223 pp.

Nearly seventy excellent color plates of antique pile carpets of Afshār, Bakhtiyāri, Khamseh, Lor, and Qashqā'i provenance. Numerous other plates of *gelim* and *suzanduzi* weavings and single and double bags, salt bags, *mafresh*, and decorative items for quadrupeds.

Oriental Rug Review, 1981–.

Features monthly surveys of "Oriental Rugs at Auction" and "The Current Market." Deserves regular perusal for occasional noteworthy articles on technical and cultural aspects of Persian carpets.

Parhām, Bāqer. "Honar va San'at-e Qālibāfi" [Art and Craft of Carpet-weaving]. *Nāmeh-ye 'Olum-e Ejtemā'i* 1, no. 2 (Winter 1968): 150–165.

Parhām, Sirus. *Qāli-ye Bolvardi* [The Bolvardi Carpet]. Tehran: Franklin Books, 1973. 56 pp.

An important study of a Qashqā'i-related tribal carpet type, with color plates of classical antique examples.

Pope, Arthur Upham, et al. "The Art of Persian Carpet Making." In *A Survey of Persian Art, from Prehistoric Times to the Present*, vol. 3, pp. 2257–2465; vol. 6, pp. 1107–1275 (plates). New York: Oxford University Press, 1939.

A standard discussion of history, the technique of Persian carpet weaving, and materials used in the making of carpets. Important color plates of classical antique pieces. Recent editions include material from a 1960 international conference.

The Qashqa'i of Iran. London: World of Islam Festival, 1976. 95 pp., 45 plates. Exhibition catalogue.

Reed, Stanley. *All Color Book of Oriental Carpets and Rugs*. New York: Crescent, 1972. 72 pp.

Color plates of mostly nineteenth-century Arāk, Bakhtiyāri, Esfahān, Farāhān, Heris, Kāshān, Kermān, Khorāsān, Kurdish, Mashhad, Polonaise, Qashqā'i, Rāvar, Tabriz, and Tehrān carpets, as well as some of the world's most famous Persian carpets, i.e., the Pazyryk carpet, the Ardabil Shrine carpet, the Chelsea carpet, the Milan hunting carpet, the Vienna silk hunting carpet, the Vienna animal and floral carpet, the Milan animal and floral with medallion and inscription carpet, and the Paris (half of) animal and tree with medallion carpet.

Rudenko, Sergei. *Frozen Tombs of Siberia*. Translated by M. W. Thompson. Berkeley: University of California Press, 1970. xxxvi, 340 [+144] pp.

Includes illustrations and discussion of the Pazyryk carpet.

Sarre, Friedrich, and Hermann Trenkwald. *Oriental Carpet Designs in Full Color*. New York: Dover, 1979. 44 pp.

Forty-five plates of classical antique *afshān*, animal, arabesque medallion, garden, hunting, and vase carpets. Also the Ardabil Shrine carpet.

Schlamminger, Karl, and Peter Lamborn Wilson. *Weaver of Tales: Persian Picture Rugs/Persische Bildteppiche*. Munich: Callway, 1980. 198 pp.

Schlick, Donald P. *Modern Oriental Carpets: A Buyer's Guide*. Rutland, Vt.: C. E. Tuttle, 1970. 139 pp.

Includes a brief discussion of the "Economics of Oriental Carpet Buying," pp. 48–51, in which it is argued that fair carpet prices can be determined by multiplying the rug density times the carpet area times the carpet factor. The carpet factor for each weaving area is a decimal derived from the calculation of basic carpet features, cost of living, wages paid to weavers, etc.

Schroeder, Eric. "The Art of Looking at Rugs." In *McMullan Exhibition*, pp. 4–13. Cambridge, Mass.: Fogg Art Museum, 1949.

Schürmann, Ulrich. *Oriental Carpets*. Rev. and expand. ed. Translated by James Clark. London: Octopus, 1979. 247 pp.

Sherrill, Sarah B. "Oriental Carpets in Seventeenth- and Eighteenth-Century America." *Antiques* 109 (January–June 1976): 142–167.

Stead, Rexford. *The Ardabil Carpets*. Malibu, Calif.: J. Paul Getty Museum, 1974. 49 pp.

Includes a color plate of the Los Angeles Ardabil Shrine carpet.

Stone, Peter F. *Oriental Rug Repair*. Chicago: Green-leaf, 1981. 166 pp.
> Adequate descriptions and illustrations of repair problems and techniques. Unreliable glossary.

Sylvester, David. "On Western Attitudes to Eastern Carpets." In *Islamic Carpets from the Joseph V. McMullan Collection*, pp. 4–19. London: Arts Council of Great Britain, 1972.

Thompson, Jon. "The Anatomy of a Carpet." In *The Persian Carpet*, pp. 65–77. London: Lefevre and Partners, 1977.

Towfiq, Firuz, and Mostafā Nirumand. *Barrasi-ye San'at-e Farsh dar Irān—Mantaqeh-ye Qālibāfi-ye Kermān* [Investigation of the Craft of Carpets in Iran—The Carpetweaving Region of Kermān]. Tehrān: 1967/1968.

Tschebull, Raoul. "Antique Lori Pile Weaving." *Hali* 1 (1978): 37–38.

Varzi, Mansur. *Honar va San'at-e Qāli dar Irān* [The Art and Industry of Carpets in Iran]. Tehrān: Raz, 1971. 315 pp.
> Study of the history of dyes, designs, and carpetweaving.

Weiss, Jeffrey. *Rugs*. Photography by David Leach and Jon Elliott. New York: Norton, 1979. 94 pp.
> One hundred sixty-three color plates of flat weave and pile rugs, mostly with furniture in room settings, including Arāk, Heris, Kermān, Kurdish, Mahāl, Qashqā'i, Rāvar, Tabriz, and Torkaman carpets.

Wulff, Hans E. *The Traditional Crafts of Persia: Their Development, Technology, and Influence on Western Civilizations*. Cambridge, Mass.: MIT Press, 1966. xxiv, 404 pp.

Yetkin, Şerare. "Iranian Influence on Caucasian Carpets." In *Early Caucasian Carpets in Turkey* (2 vols.), translated by Arlette and Alan Mellaarts, vol. 1, pp. 90–104. Atlantic Highlands, N.J.: Humanities Press, 1978.

Index